T0326473

The Rise and Fall of the Privatized Pension System in Chile

The Rise and Fall of the Privatized Pension System in Chile

An International Perspective

Andrés Solimano

ANTHEM PRESS

Anthem Press
An imprint of Wimbledon Publishing Company
www.anthempress.com

This edition first published in UK and USA 2021
by ANTHEM PRESS
75–76 Blackfriars Road, London SE1 8HA, UK
or PO Box 9779, London SW19 7ZG, UK
and
244 Madison Ave #116, New York, NY 10016, USA

Copyright © Andrés Solimano 2021

The author asserts the moral right to be identified as the author of this work.

All rights reserved. Without limiting the rights under copyright reserved above,
no part of this publication may be reproduced, stored or introduced into
a retrieval system, or transmitted, in any form or by any means
(electronic, mechanical, photocopying, recording or otherwise),
without the prior written permission of both the copyright
owner and the above publisher of this book.

British Library Cataloguing-in-Publication Data
A catalogue record for this book is available from the British Library.

Library of Congress Control Number: 2021931846

ISBN-13: 978-1-78527-356-8 (Hbk)
ISBN-10: 1-78527-356-6 (Hbk)

This title is also available as an e-book.

CONTENTS

ACKNOWLEDGMENTS

This book corresponds to an expanded and updated version of my book *Pensiones a la Chilena* published in Spanish. The present version, was translated into English by Pedro Solimano. The English edition incorporates a more detailed historical analysis of the evolution of social security laws in Chile since the 19th century, new data on pension levels of the civilian population and the armed force personnel along with new material on the use of pension savings to fund economic conglomerates. Marco Kremerman from Fundacion Sol in Santiago provided useful comments to the whole manuscript. Effective research assistance provided by Damian Gildemeister and Francisca Barriga is much appreciated. I would also like to express my thanks to Megan Geiving, senior editor at Anthem Press, and the production team headed by Jayashree for their permanent and effective support in the publication of this book.

Chapter 1

INTRODUCTION

From the 1980s to the 2010s, we have witnessed a cycle of privatization and then de-privatization of pension systems that reached nearly 30 countries, mostly in Latin America and Central and Eastern Europe. Chile privatized its pension system in the Pinochet regime in the early 1980s and at the time of this writing it is still stuck with that system. The promise of pension systems based on individual accounts administered by financial companies were multiple and ambitious: higher pensions, lower burdens on the fiscal budget, private saving mobilization, individual choice, depoliticization of pension policies and higher rates of economic growth. After a few decades of application of capitalization pillars, the reality was far more disappointing than the promise at the outset of the privatization experiment in a number of countries. This privatized pension model had been recommended by international financial institutions, free market economists and private financial institutions that perceived large pools of resources to be intermediated for profit. However, the new reality was of low pension benefits, high fees charged by pension management companies, enlarged fiscal deficits, low coverage, financial volatility, lack of social participation in the management of pension funds and the redirection of the workers' pension savings funds to finance the operations of large corporations, commercial banks and economic conglomerates. In light of these realities, with differences across economies, nearly 20 countries chose to *de-privatize* their pension systems (partially or completely) and return to public pension systems. Mandatory private pillars were significantly downsized or closed in the counterreform process. In contrast, mature capitalist economies did not choose the radical privatization route in response to the various demographic challenges of an aging population, fiscal constraints and productivity slowdowns faced by high per capita income nations. These nations introduced adjustments to the benefits of their social security systems and increased retirement ages but without abandoning the social contract of intergenerational solidarity and progressive redistribution that lies at the foundation of modern social security systems.

The purpose of this book is to examine the pension privatization experience of Chile, placing it in a proper historical and international perspective.

This country embarked during an authoritarian regime in the full privatization of its pension system for the civilian population. Due to its peculiar political and economic circumstances of the early 1980s, Chile became an earlier pension privatizer. Despite that this system has been socially contested by the Chilean population, its private pension model has been presented, internationally, as a success story for other countries to follow. In contrast to other nations, in Chile, the privatized system has remained in place for nearly four decades in spite of its record of low pensions, gender biases, high profits of the pension management industry and regressive saving redistribution from labor to big capital. The ultimate fate of the system inherited from the Pinochet regime and maintained in place by seven civilian governments afterward is still unclear, although it is under strong social criticism and contestation. The political economy of reform shows the interplay, conflict and tensions between two opposing camps: on the one hand, the labor movement and the working class, civil society organizations, middle-income people and the impoverished elderly all of them pushing for fundamental re-reform in the direction of a publicly based system and, on the other hand, the strong resistance—helped by the conservative mass media, largely dominant in Chile—to change by the powerful lobby of the pension intermediation industry that exerts direct influence on mainstream economists, financial experts, politicians, hesitant center-right and center-left governments and a largely accommodative parliament.

The Chilean Experience

In the 19th century, Chile developed rudimentary mechanisms of social protection based on the action of associations of mutual help, the philanthropic initiatives of the church and emerging labor unions. The early 20th century was a period of increasing activism of the working classes that pushed for new labor legislation on basic labor rights, regulation of work hours, child labor, working holiday on Sundays and so on. The first formal social security scheme was born in 1915 for the army and the navy. Railway workers also got access to social protection in the 1910s. In 1924–25, following a complex period of social unrest, political instability and military unrest, new social legislation was approved by congress establishing social protection boards for manual workers (Caja de Seguro Obrero), public sector employees and journalists (Caja de Empleados Públicos y Periodistas) and for private sector (white collar) employees (Caja de Empleados Particulares). In the late 1920s, the Ministry of Labor was created during the first presidency of General Carlos Ibañez del Campo. Later, pension schemes were set for specific occupations such as the merchant navy, commerce, racetracks and others. As Chile embraced a development strategy of import substitution industrialization, with the state broadening the provision of social services to the middle-class and urban workers, social security (health, pensions, at-work accident prevention and cure) expanded, and a national health system was established in 1952. The breadth and scope of the social security boards created in 1924–25 were also enhanced in subsequent decades until the military coup of 1973.

Chile was one of the leaders in Latin America to introduce social security in the 20th century. Benefits were expanded to broad segments of the population and the *cajas* (social security boards) were participatory in their management under tripartite schemes with presence of representatives of employees, employers and the state. At the same time, the pension boards displayed substantial heterogeneity in rules and eligibility criteria across occupations, the real value of monetary benefits was vulnerable to inflation and the financial solvency of the *cajas* was not always robust. Reform attempts of social security were undertaken by different governments, on some occasions with the help of foreign advisors. Some of them were more concerned with macro stabilization, as was the case with the Klein-Sachs mission (a private team of "money doctors") brought in by the second government of Carlos Ibañez del Campo in the 1950s to stop inflation and reduce fiscal deficits. Other advisors were national such as the Prat Commission (led by the Chilean lawyer Jorge Prat) in the early 1960s; this commission was appointed by the conservative government of Jorge Alessandri-Rodriguez (son of former president Arturo Alessandri Palma). In turn, the administration of President Frei Montalva (Christian Democrat) in the second half of the 1960s and the Allende government (socialist) in the early 1970s also presented to parliament reform plans that combined expansion of benefits with administrative and financial reforms of social security bodies. The different attempts at pension reform had shown that achieving political consensus in this area was far from easy to attain and actual progress in improving social security was stalled.

The military regime that ousted by force the democratically elected government of President Salvador Allende on September 11, 1973, and that ruled iron-fist for 17 years, also wanted to reform social security. After an initial flirting with national-corporatist policies, the authoritarian regime engaged in a neoliberal revolution oriented to reshape the Chilean economy and society along "free market" lines. Regarding social security, corporatists and neoliberals clashed. In 1975, the Ministry of Labor and Social Security, dominated by the air force and led by General Nicolas Diaz Estrada (an organizer, along with Augusto Pinochet, of the military coup of September 1973), presented a neo-corporatist proposal to reform the social security system to the military junta. The junta was formed by the commanders of the army, air force, navy and Carabineros (a militarized national police) and acted as the legislative body of the country replacing the national congress, that was suspended in its operation the same day of the military coup and remained closed for 17 years thereafter. The draft law proposed the creation of social security corporations (coporaciones de seguridad social) that would be not-for-profit agencies managed by workers through their labor unions (most of them already decimated by the repression of the new military regime). In a new twist, individual accounts would be introduced. The financing of pension and other health benefits was to rest on a mix of pay-as-you-go funding rules and capitalization schemes. In the corporatist model promoted by the air force, revamped social security would follow, at least on paper, the principles of the International Labor Office (e.g., tripartite contributions, workers participation and social dialogue, financial sustainability and others). Nevertheless, the principles of workers participation in the management of social security entities and the not-for-profit character did not convince the free market economists already appointed to top positions in the government by General Pinochet.

At the end, in 1980, the free market technocracy helped by the removal of the corporatists of the air force from government[1] convinced the military junta to adopt a fully privatized pension system in Chile, at least for the civilian population. The new system was centered by individual pension savings accounts managed by profit-maximizing companies (the Administradoras de Fondos de Pensiones, AFP by its Spanish acronyms) run by financial officers. Moreover, workers' presence in the board of directors of the AFP was neither envisaged nor promoted. The rule of capital was secured and the workers' run Corporaciones de Seguridad Social recommended by the nationalists of the air force were removed from consideration. It is important to note that the new pension system was a big policy gamble—an experiment in social engineering—as no precedent of *privatized* social security existed in the world. The only country at the time that had a system of individual accounts in social security was Singapore, which was fully administered by the state. The fact that Chile was a high inequality country in which workers earned modest wages in a scheme that was crucially dependent on the saving potential of the population was overlooked. The gamble was that the magic of compound interest rates, high in the 1980s but not in subsequent decades, would make their savings grow at rapid pace ensuring, therefore, good pensions at retirement.

---

[1] This also coincided with the dissent of the commander in chief of the air force, also a co-organizer of the coup of 1973, General Gustavo Leigh, on the growing neoliberal orientation of the regime and the perpetuation in power of General Pinochet. This led, eventually, to the removal of Leigh and several generals, including Diaz-Estrada, from the government.

The traditional principles of intergenerational solidarity and redistribution within generations that guide most social security systems were replaced by a new ethic of "individual responsibility." Now, each wage earner must look after himself or herself, trying to get a well-paid job and making sure that every month they keep contributing to their individual pension accounts. In this new world of individual accounts, contributors had to make complex financial choices on the return-risk combination of their pension funds, a task not easy even for a well-trained financial specialist.

The history of how the current pension system came into existence is telling of the power structure prevailing in Chile in the early 1980s under the military rule. After some discussion on the merits and also potential risks of adopting an *untried* privatized social security system, the military persuaded General Pinochet to adopt the capitalization system *only for the civilian population.* For the armed forces, the existing social security system based on generous contributions from the state was to remain in place. Therefore, the personnel of the army, navy, air force, Carabineros, investigative police and the staff of the jail system were released of the obligation to contribute to the new system of pensions based on individual accounts managed by private financial companies. Their system was to continue to be administered by the own pension system of the armed forces and national police (CAPREDENA and DIPRECA by their Spanish acronym) and receiving generous transfers from the state.[2]

On October 14, 1980, a *secret session* of the military junta was convened to decide on the new pension system for Chile. In that session, it was approved the decree-law # 3,500 that enabled the privatization of the pension system and granted the *monopoly* of managing the individual accounts to the AFP (see Chapter 5). Shortly afterward, the decree was published in the Diario Oficial (Official Gazette) and the system started its operation in 1981.

At the time of this writing, nearly four decades later, the AFP system still retains the monopoly on the pension individual accounts, reaching 11 million affiliates that could not choose any other pension scheme (since 1981, no pay-as-you-go option was available to the new entrants to the workforce in Chile). It is worth noting that a host of civilian governments (both of center-left and center-right persuasions) that have alternated in office after the departure of the Pinochet regime in 1990 have refrained from attempting to end the monopoly of the AFP on the individual accounts.

Interestingly, the Chilean private pension system imposed by the military and its free market technocracy was promoted for years, with the help from international financial institutions (World Bank, the Inter-American

---

[2] CAPREDENA (Caja de Prevision de la Defensa Nacional) and DIPRECA (Dirección de Previsión de Carabineros).

Development Bank, OECD and others)[3] as a role model for other countries to emulate. As examined in this book (Chapter 4), there was a wave of privatization of pension systems in Latin America and Central and Eastern Europe that started in the 1990s (in Chile in the early 1980s) and early 2000s but that was followed by a subsequent de-privatization in a number of countries (Argentina, Bolivia, Poland, Hungary, Czech Republic, Slovakia, Russia and others) in the mid- to late 2000s and in the 2010s. These countries had jumped into the privatization fever of the 1990s following optimistic promises unbacked by hard evidence. The Chilean system, itself in its infancy in the 1990s and still dominated by a phase of resource accumulation with very few actual pensioners, was viewed as the blueprint for pension reform.

Another mechanism for inducing countries to adopt capitalization schemes was through loan conditionality by the Bretton Woods institutions and regional development banks. Borrowing countries were compelled to adopt as "prior conditions" for receiving structural adjustment loans and technical assistance to present to their parliament plans to introduce capitalization schemes run by the private sector replacing public sector-based social security. Loan disbursements, in turn, were also conditional on actual progress (decrees and laws) in implementing the privatization of social security.

For the local and international financial sector, the introduction of individual accounts managed by the private (capitalist) sector was a very interesting proposition. Now, with new laws, growing volumes of compulsory financial savings of workers and employees could be intermediated, at a profit (commission), and channeled into local capital markets for investment in companies, banks and the national treasury-issuing bonds, equity and other financial instruments. This proved to be a source of low-cost financing to big business, economic conglomerates and commercial banks and also helped to cover part of the fiscal deficit originated by the transition to the new system.

The Structure of the Privatized Chilean Pension System

The Chilean pension system is structured around four subsystems (pillars). The main pillar is composed of the AFP and insurance companies that as of early 2020 manage nearly US$ 220 billion in pension funds (the GDP is about US$ 300 billion).[4] The other three subsystems are (i) the "solidarity pillar,"

---

[3] The International Monetary Fund was more guarded in this regard since it was aware of the adverse effects on public finances that this privatization would entail.

[4] As of October of 2020, the total fund declined to nearly US$ 195,000 following authorizations to withdraw up to 10 percent of their pension funds holdings by affiliates to help to cope with the economic effects of Covid-19.

a state-run basic pension tier, that pays a: (a) basic pension to low-income people that generally do not make regular contributions to the pension funds and (b) a supplement pension subsidy to affiliates earning low pensions in the privatized pillar. These two benefits are directly funded by fiscal revenues (rentas generales de la nacion); (ii) the Social Security Institute (IPS for its Spanish acronym) manages pensions of those who remained affiliated in the old social security system (the old *cajas*) that ceased to exist in 1981. The IPS also manages payments of several benefits of the solidarity pillar; and (iii) a state-supported public pension system for the army, air force, navy and the national police and investigative police (CAPREDENA and DIPRECA). The first three pillars (AFP and insurance companies, solidarity pillar, IPS) serve the civilian population and the fourth pillar pertains to the national defense sector.

The financing of public pension expenditure between the public and private sectors is very unbalanced. Nearly two-thirds of total pension spending is made by the public sector, while the private pillar (AFP and insurance companies) make-up for only one-third of the pension outlays of the system, although they control 11 million accounts, by far the largest pillar in terms of affiliates.

The average pension benefits received by retired members of the armed forces and national policy (c. 2016–19) are about *four to five times higher* than the average pensions paid by the AFP/insurance companies to the civilian population (Chapter 5). These big differences in benefits between segments of the national system of social security are clearly inconsistent with the organizing principles, embedded in treaties, directives and recommendations made by the United Nations through the International Labor Organization (ILO) to member governments regarding uniformity of benefits for equivalent contributions across subsystems of social security.

The pillar of private capitalization mobilizes such a large volume of pension savings from wage earners that they cannot be absorbed, entirely, by the local capital market. Therefore, the paradox is that a middle-income country with savings needs manages to *export out of the country* nearly 45 percent of total pension funds that are invested outside Chile through the pension system. Proponents of the capitalization system argue that this contributes to the diversification of the pension funds by reducing their exposure to negative internal shocks. This argument would be certain if local and international capital markets were uncorrelated in their returns. However, the international experience since the 1980s, with frequent national, regional and global financial crisis that are generally correlated through contagion effects, deprives this argument of practical validity.

Another feature of the pension industry in Chile is increasing *denationalization*. Since the decade of the 2010s, pension fund management companies (AFP) have been controlled by international insurance and financial consortiums such as American conglomerates Metlife and Principal Financial Group, and the Colombian Sura group. In turn, these companies are organized into the Asociación de AFP, an owner-association, that advances the interests of the pension management companies. Apparently, this organization manages substantial budgets that are spent in lobby activities, the funding of pro-AFP campaigns in the mass media, the organization of seminars and the contacting of policy makers and politicians in order to influence their law initiatives and voting in parliament, making efforts to prevent any legislation that could undermine their financial and corporate interests.

The intermediation of pension funds in Chile is an extremely profitable niche from a commercial perspective. This activity is subject to no state-imposed ceilings on the fees charged by the AFPs to the owners of individual accounts (workers). The average rate of return on invested capital (ROI) by the AFP system was 22 percent for the period 2004–18, exceeding the significantly high profit rates of the Chilean banking sector (enjoying stiff entry barriers) and exceed, by far, the estimates of the social rate of return of physical capital in the Chilean economy that is closer to 8 percent. A disturbing feature of the capitalization system from the viewpoint of ensuring a stable income profile of future pensions is that pension funds are invested in volatile capital markets. At a more general level, this is an inescapable characteristic of the capital markets in a capitalist economy as highlighted by noted economists of the 20th century such as John Maynard Keynes and Hyman Minsky. Financial shocks and crises do affect the value of the pension-wealth of affiliates and, therefore, their stream of pensions at retirement, hitting more severely to affiliates whose funds are invested in risky funds. The system is divided in five funds according to their risk-return profiles with Funds A and B investing mainly in domestic and foreign stocks (potentially more volatile), and Funds C, D and E funds are invested, in greater proportion, in fixed income instruments. Furthermore, the pensioners are not only exposed to financial risk but also face the so-called longevity risk (unexpected lower pensions because of extended lives) triggered when pension funds in the individual accounts run out of funds because of previous pension payments.

Around two-thirds of the pension funds invested in Chile are directed to serve the financial needs of commercial banks, large corporations and investment banks and other financial intermediaries (Chapter 5). The use of pension funds to finance large economic conglomerates contributes to the concentration of ownership of the capital stock of the economy in the hands of small economic conglomerates and wealthy elites. As small- and medium-sized enterprises—that generate a large proportion of employment in the economy and create incomes for the middle class and the working class—do not issue the financial instruments (stocks and bonds) acquired by the AFPs, they do not have access to the savings pool generated by workers and appropriated by the pension funds.

The Battle for Pension Reform and the Blocking of Change

The sociopolitical dynamics of the consolidation of the private capitalization system in Chile underscores the power of entrenched interests such as the lobby of the AFP to avert fundamental reforms that could undermine their monopoly over millions of individual accounts. The AFP use various mechanisms for leveraging influence on executive and legislative powers in Chile. These mechanisms include the appointment of former government ministers in their board of directors, the financing of political campaigns of congressmen, the launching of pro-AFP campaigns in the media, the hiring of economists and financial experts to show the "virtues" of private capitalization and other initiatives. The system, however, has been contested both by social security experts without ties with the pension industry and by social and labor organizations, chiefly the *Coordinadora de Trabajadores No + AFP movement*. This is a broad collation of workers union and other social organizations critical of the privatized pension system. The leader of the movement (formally his spokesman in a horizontal organization) is Mr. Luis Mesina, the head of the union of commercial banking officers. The *Coordinadora de Trabajadores No + AFP* movement runs on a well-targeted platform: abolish the private capitalization system run by the AFP and replace it by a genuine social security system around principles of intergenerational solidarity and redistribution. Their pledge has been echoed greatly among the population. Mass rallies against the current pension system have been able to convene, in certain occasions, millions of citizens throughout the country. An important trait of the No + AFP movement that renders credibility to its demands is its full independence from political parties and the government.

The legitimacy of the private pension system has been further undermined by the contrast between the meager pensions paid by the private pillar and the high profit rates earned by the pension management companies. Another contentious issue is the contrast between the generous benefits granted to the pension system of national defense and the low pension receiving the bulk of the civilian population contributing to the private pension management companies. Another feature of the pension system in Chile is its absence of *systemic choice* faced by the affiliates. In spite of the fact that the Chilean economy is presented as a model of free market economics, in the realm of pensions its citizens *do not* have the freedom to choose between publicly provided or privately provided pensions schemes. Any new entrant to the workforce and the labor market who is offered a contract by an employer, ought, by law, to make a social security contribution only to a *private* pension management provider. This is inimical to the principles of economic liberalism promoted by Milton Friedman and Friedrich Hayek (both highly influential in shaping economic policies in Chile) that at least in theory, promoted choice and competition.

Partial Reforms

Interestingly, and indicative of the way the Chilean democracy works, at the time of this writing, no civilian government after the Pinochet period has ever tried to revoke the law (the DL 3,500) that created the current pension system in 1980 that was approved by a military junta rather than by an elected parliament. A concrete example of refraining from any substantial challenge to the AFP monopoly over the pension management industry is the so-called pension reform of 2008. This reform was undertaken under the first presidency of social-democrat Ms. Michelle Bachelet and written into Law 20,225. Actually, what was presented as a "fundamental reform in the pension system" amounted to the creation of a pillar of basic, non-contributing, pensions, the *Pilar Solidario* that was not created in 1980 and that was largely needed given the incidence of poverty among the elderly. However, the dominant contributory pillar of capitalization was left virtually intact, completely in the hands of the AFP fully preserving the scheme introduced by the Pinochet regime. In fact, no pension management company run by the state (e.g., a public AFP) was allowed to exist after the "reforms of 2008" and decree 3,500 continued into operation. Furthermore, no reviewing of the fiscally expensive national defense pension system was undertaken by the two pension reform commissions appointed by President Bachelet in her two governments (2006–10 and 2014–18). Amendments to the system focused on the introduction of some additional child benefits, the auctioning of new entrant portfolios and the super-intendency of AFP was renamed as Super-intendency of Pensions entitled with some new functions.

In the second government of President Bachelet some partial reforms to make employers to contribute to social security were presented to parliament but time ran out for approval before the end of her government and the second Piñera government increased, partially, resources to the Solidarity Pillar but has chosen to leave the private contributory pillar largely unchanged (Chapter 6).

Organization of the Book

This book is organized in six chapters, including this introduction.

In Chapter 2, we present the logic of social security as a collective mechanism (a social contract) to cope with risks such as unemployment, work accidents, job disability, death of the main income-earner in a household and income support at old age. The chapter compares pay-as-you-go systems with capitalization and traces the origins of public social security in European countries, such as Von Bismarck's Germany in the 1880s, the adoption of social insurance in other European countries, the creation of the International Labor Office in 1919, the federal social security system in the United States in the 1930s and the rise of social security schemes in Latin American countries in the 20th century. Chapter 3 examines the cycle of privatization and subsequent de-privatization of pension systems in several countries of Latin America and Central and Eastern Europe that cover from the 1980s (Chile as the starter) to the de-privatizations in Rumania in 2017. The chapter reviews country experiences of *reversal* of the privatization that started around the time of the 2008 financial crisis and continued thereafter. The cases of de-privatization in Argentina, Hungary and Poland are discussed in detail. These reversals were motivated by several failures of the new system such as the deterioration of pension benefits, high fees charged by pension fund management companies and, very importantly, fiscal imbalances associated with the introduction of individual accounts and the fall of contributions to the public pillar.

Chapter 4 presents a historical account of the creation and evolution of social insurance in Chile from the 19th century to the 1980s when the pension system is privatized. The chapter provides detailed information on labor and social security laws passed throughout the 20th century in response to increasing social activism by labor unions surrounded by periods of social mobilization, political instability and changing development strategies and social policies. The chapter also documents the controversies within the military regime of general Pinochet between the national-corporatists and the neoliberal economists before full privatization for the civilian population was adopted in a secret session of the military junta in October 1980. In that session General Pinochet and other army generals expressed their doubts on the convenience of privatizing social security but ultimately decided to go ahead with the privatization plan of the neoliberal economic team while safeguarding the armed forces that remained in a public pension system with generous benefits.

Chapter 5 evaluates the optimistic promises made at the outset of the privatization experiment regarding high replacement rates, isolation from political pressures, efficiency, enhanced choice by workers and the lowering of fiscal costs under a privatized system. The chapter notes how Pinochet's economic team underestimated (or disregarded) the enormous concentration of economic and political power that the newly born AFP lobby would entail following the control of a growing savings pool coming from pension's contributions. The chapter presents updated empirical evidence on the level of pensions, differences of benefits between the various subsystems, the high profit rates of the AFPs and the allocation of pension funds toward commercial banks, big corporations, the national treasury and economic conglomerates that form a sort of private–public consortium benefitting from the low-cost financing coming from the pension system. It also discusses macro, sector and political economy mechanisms to keep the capitalist private sector (as different from small- and medium-sized enterprises) capture of the pension system.

Chapter 6 presents the main findings of the book, mentions the partial reform attempts to introduce some solidarity elements into a privatized pension system and outlines a proposal for *de-privatization* of the current pension system in Chile that entails abolishing law 3,500 of 1980 that enables the legal monopoly of the pension fund management companies (AFPs) on the pension system and creating a modern PAYG pillar that can coexist with a smaller and more competitive capitalization pillar, within a system operating under internationally accepted principles of social security.

Chapter 2

AN OVERVIEW OF SOCIAL SECURITY: PURPOSES, MODALITIES AND HISTORICAL EVOLUTION

2.1 Purposes and Modalities

Social security systems develop mechanisms to cope with uncertainties, unexpected shocks and disruptions that affect working people and those who are retired from the workforce. In the economist's jargon, a properly working social security system should help smooth consumption from a variety of adverse shocks and changes in life cycle circumstances. People face risks such as losing their jobs, accidents at the workplace, sickness and disabilities and getting old and therefore turning less suitable to continue an active working life. They may also face the death of the main income earner that creates hardship and eventually leads to family dissolution. The shocks felt at individual and household levels may be associated with macroeconomic and financial crises that create unemployment, bankruptcy of firms and skill mismatches. Other sources of risk are associated with the propagation of pathogens (pandemics) and natural disasters such as earthquakes, floods and hurricanes, climate change, war and armed conflict.

A comprehensive list of relevant risks, whose consequences the mechanisms of social protection and social security try to prevent or compensate, includes:

- (i)   occupational accidents and sickness,
- (ii)   disability,
- (iii)   death of the main income provider or head of household,
- (iv)   the loss of a job and the entering to the unemployment pool,
- (v)   old age,
- (vi)   impact of natural disasters such as earthquakes, floods and hurricanes,
- (vi)   effects of an armed conflict or wars,
- (vii)   the effects of a pandemic.

Historically, before the advent of state-sponsored social security to cope with these contingencies, the church, philanthropic organizations, societies of friendship and mutual help and labor unions were important sources of support for those affected by adverse shocks and risks. In general, these mechanisms were funded through member contributions, monetary donations by wealthy families, male and female voluntary work in charitable and solidarity-oriented organizations. The eruption of government-sponsored social insurance was, many times, motivated by the pressure and mobilization of working-class organizations affected by rapid industrialization, technical change that replaced labor for machinery and equipment, the intensification of labor intensity in the factory system through extending working hours, the use of child labor in capitalist production, job losses due to import penetration and outward foreign direct investment. In the capitalist core countries, these trends took place mainly during the late 18th and 19th centuries, while in the countries of the periphery of the world economy this process occurred mainly in the 20th and early 21st centuries, following intensified economic globalization and technological revolutions.

At a conceptual level, social risks can be faced at three levels:

a. Privately (individual or family level);
b. At community level through labor unions, societies of mutual help, the church and charitable organizations; and
c. State-sponsored social security.

At an individual/household level, building personal/family savings pool can be a precautionary strategy to face social risks and old age vulnerabilities. A person can open a savings account at a bank to have resources to face the financial costs of sickness, unemployment and other contingencies. The individual may also choose to buy a property, put it on rent and receive an income stream that will help cope with adverse contingencies.[1] In turn, a person can go to an insurance company and buy an "annuity" delivering a monthly income flow after retirement standing until death. It is important to note that the strategy of building personal savings and portfolio allocations require a degree of financial preparation that most individuals may not possess. On the other hand, very importantly, their income profile may prevent them from building a savings pool.

---

[1] A chief economist of the Bank of England (the oldest central bank in the world), Andy Haldane, has recommended the acquisition of property (whose price tends to increase in the medium term) as a better alternative than a pension to ensure an income source during retirement (*The Guardian*, August 28, 2016).

Additionally, having an *extended family* (rearing several children and developing close ties with uncles, aunts and cousins) is another way of facing risks that historically was very important. In fact, households may choose to have many children who may take care of their parents at old age or in case of accidents or serious illness. More recently, during the austerity policies applied in Greece in the 2010s, when youth unemployment climbed over 50 percent, many young Greeks who had lost their jobs returned to live with their parents who were receiving respectable state-funded pensions.[2] Therefore, the family—helped by a working social security system—can be a very important source of support in the event of adverse labor market and health shocks.

The logic of individual saving, valuable as it is, as a *main* mechanism for coping with social risks and pension generation presents at least two main limitations:

a. In many economies, particularly in developing nations, important segments of the population have a very limited savings capacity[3] due to low wages, chronic underemployment and lack of job opportunities. Therefore, the ability to build an asset base during their working life to finance retirement will be constrained, resulting in vulnerability and poverty at old age.

b. Myopic behavior and a tendency to see retirement as too far ahead on time[4] or underestimate the occurrence of adverse shocks and large-scale calamities may lead to the failure of building an adequate asset base to face contingencies. Economists may refer to this as "irrational behavior" or having "high discount rates" to refer to situations in which people value significantly more current consumption than future consumption. In addition, probability analysis may simply fail: long ago, the British economist John Maynard Keynes pointed out in his *Treatise on Probability* the existence of "fundamental uncertainty," as different from ordinal risk, referring to the fact that for a certain range of events (a pandemic, a war, climate change and so forth) individuals have no way to imagine or assign probabilities to their realization.

---

[2] Solimano (2017).

[3] Empirical studies for several medium- to high-income countries show that only the richest 10 percent of the population is capable of obtaining financial assets in a systematic way and that the poorest 40 percent never accumulate financial wealth during their working lives. See Solimano (2017).

[4] A young person entering the workforce may see no urgency to start savings 40–50 years before retirement.

2.1.1 Pension systems as a social contract: The pay-as-you-go modality

As already mentioned, public social security systems arose in the late 19th century as a *collective answer* to the existence of social risks and old age support needs. Leaving protection to these risks only to individual decisions and/or to charity organizations and mutual aid societies could condemn workers and their families to the hazards of sickness, unemployment, disabilities and old age precariousness. Under these conditions, the state should consider as *social rights* of its citizens having social protection to face with adverse contingencies in the workplace and other health contingencies. The German model inaugurated by Von Bismarck, then extended to other countries, was based on an implicit social contract of *intergenerational solidarity* in the case of old age pensions payments. The contract was simple: current generation of workers and employees (the "active population") pay an excise on their earnings that is used to finance the pensions of today's pensioners (the "passive population") in the understanding that future pensioners will be funded by the future active workers. This is the essence of a *pay-as-you-go pension system* based on an intergenerational transfer.

The scheme can (or cannot) have a reserve fund that guarantees payments to the retiree for a certain period in case there is a disruption in the flow of payment by the active population due to, for example, unemployment. This system depends, crucially, on several parameters such as the ratio of active workers to retirees, life expectancy at the age of retirement, the growth rate of total wages and the rate of contribution to the pension system.

In terms of reach, coverage and financing structure, historically we can distinguish two main pay-as you-go pensions models:[5]

i.   *Corporate-contributive model* (the German Bismarckian model), based on the monetary contributions of workers and companies, with supplementary support from the state. The Bismarckian (tripartite) model was largely adopted by the International Labor Office (ILO) created in 1919 in the aftermath of World War I and recommended for its member countries.

ii.   The *universalist model* (Beveridge System) in which pension and other social benefits are financed out of general revenues of the state. This model was incorporated as the basis for the welfare state in Britain devised by

---

[5] The author Esping-Andersen (1996), in his taxonomy on welfare states in Europe, referred to this scheme as "conservative-corporative" (Continental Europe). His other two categories were the "social-democratic welfare State" (Nordic countries) and the "European liberal welfare system" in place in the United Kingdom.

William Beveridge in the early 1940s. The model intends as beneficiaries the whole population of a country, "from the cradle to the grave" as the motto in Britain in the welfare state designed by Beveridge, in that sense is "universalist."

The United States adopted (rather late, compared to Europe) a *federal* social security system in the 1930s, motivated by the high social costs of the Great Depression insufficiently protected by existing local and state institutions. In turn, several Latin American countries created their own social security systems in the 1920s, although it was not until the 1940s and 1950s that this trend gained further strength.

2.1.2 *Demographic challenges*

Social security is affected by shifts in demography. In recent decades, there have been important changes to the demographic structure of the population, associated with progress in medicine and health services that reduce fertility and infant mortality rates. As a result of these trends, there is a lowering in birth rates and an increase in life expectancy. Families now have fewer children due to the incorporation of women to the labor force, higher divorce rates and the growth of single-parent homes. Lower birth rates reduce, over time, the number of people entering the workforce decreasing contributions to pension scheme. In turn, higher life expectancy makes people live longer, with the impending financial impact going on pension expenditure and old age health spending. These two tendencies create pressures on the level of benefits social security systems can afford (this reduces the ratios between active workers who contribute and passive retirees who receive pensions). It is important to recognize that pension and social security systems were created in the late 19th and early 20th centuries when the demographic trends of countries were very different from now: large contingents coming from the countryside incorporated to the workforce and the state of medicine and the reach of public health systems entailed a lower life expectancy (45–50 years old in the early 20th century in the advanced economies of that time). Now, a combination of more savings, a larger number of contributors and higher contribution rates is required in order to finance a longer-living population that face higher medical costs.

It is important to realize that demographic factors (lower fertility rates and higher life expectancy) affect both pay-as-you-go and private capitalization systems. Under both systems, earlier generations will have to contribute more and/or save more to finance benefits at old age. On one hand, in the pay-as-you-go system, lower fertility/higher life expectancy reduces the ratio of contributors to retirees, a key parameter for the solvency of the system. On the other hand, in the capitalization system, a larger stock of accumulated funds (the balance of the individual accounts at retirement) will be needed to cover the pensions of people who live longer after retirement. The capitalization system will adjust through lower pensions to the change in demography if some parameters are not changed. A similar adjustment may take place in the pay-as-you-go system unless contribution rates rise and retirement age is extended.

There is a large literature comparing pay-as-you-go and capitalization systems regarding the level of pensions, administration costs, degree of intergenerational solidarity, effects on national savings, distribution of income and other dimensions.[6]

2.1.3 Defined contributions and defined benefits

An important distinction in pension systems is between systems of defined benefits (pensions) and defined contributions (payments to social security). In general, pay-as-you-go systems are considered as defined benefits systems: the contributor knows that if he or she contributes a certain number of years, he or she will have a certain replacement rate (ratio of pension to last salaries). In the defined benefit systems, the retiree needs to know his last salary, the number of years he or she contributed and the entitled replacement rate. In contrast, in capitalization systems, the person knows with certainty what is the contribution rate to the pension fund (defined contribution) but does not know the replacement rate that will depend on the size of the accumulated funds during the working life of the pensioner that, in turn, will depend on the rate of return of the investments undertaken by the pension funds and the accumulated deductions (administration fees) charged by the pension management companies.

There are also hybrid systems that combine elements of pay-as-you-go systems with variable benefits; this is the "notional accounts" system, put in place first in Sweden in the 1990s.

A properly working pension system has high replacement rates that enable the pensioner a significant continuity in his income stream between the phase of active work (in which he receives a wage) and the phase of retirement (which depends on a pension income plus the return of voluntary savings). In contrast, a poorly working pension scheme is one in which beneficiaries, after retirement, face severe declines—a discontinuity—in their incomes (due to insufficient pensions) experiencing a deterioration of living standard at old age.

---

[6] See, for example, Diamond (1993) and Orzag and Stiglitz (1999).

Box 2.1 Notional Accounts

At a conceptual level, the notional account system or "fictitious accounts" seeks to replicate at an *accounting level* within a pay-as-you-go system the individual savings account logic in a capitalization system. As far as data on contributions are available, the systems administrator (generally a state entity) credits a certain "balance"—fictitious or notional—in the *notional account* of the affiliate and this constitutes the *pension wealth* of the contributor accumulated at a certain point in time. In turn, the "notional fund" grows at an interest rate (or implicit rate of return) fixed by pension authorities. In general, the return on notional accounts equals the growth rate of the labor force plus the growth rate of real wages (equal to the growth of the wage bill) that accrue to the pension system. In this system, the pension is equal to the ratio between pension wealth and the life expectancy of the pensioner. This notional account pension system was introduced in Sweden in 1994 and it was also adopted later in Italy, Poland and Latvia.

Source: Bosch-Supan (2004).

2.1.4 Wage-labor, the self-employed and social security

Initially, contributive social security was oriented to provide benefits to workers in the wage sector of the capitalist system. In modern times, particularly in developing countries, this is often considered the *formal sector* of the economy in which firms hire labor under a legal labor contract and pay taxes and social security contributions to the state.

In developing and emerging economies, employment in the formal sector represents a fraction of total occupation, that runs from 30 to 70 percent of total employment depending on the overall level of economic development of the country. In general, low-income, poor countries tend to have larger informal sectors (smaller formal sector) than more developed economies with higher per capita incomes; in the informal sector, workers are often hired without a legal contract and rarely pay social security contributions; a similar situation occurs for the self-employed. The coverage of the pension system refers to the percentage of workers and employees that receive social security benefits and is closely linked to the degree of formalization of the labor market, the tax system and the way social security operates. At the same time, the types of jobs and structure of occupations in the economy matter for social security. Pay-as-you-go systems were created, basically, for wage workers employed in the capitalist sector and the state sector, dominant in economies like Germany and other Central European countries in the late 19th century. However, the current reality of developing countries and "emerging economies" and semi-industrial economies like Italy, for example, shows that an important share of economic activity is generated by the self-employed, small shops and microenterprises. These units, in turn, comprise a wide range of occupations such as informal workers, artisans, family helpers, lawyers, architects, medical doctors, street vendors, in-house workers, restaurant waiters, fisherman, gardeners, and others. This array of activities may be "formal" or "informal" in the sense of the prevalence of legal incorporation of business, use of labor contracts, regularity in the payment of taxes and contributions to social security.[7]

2.1.5 Volatility in financial markets

Capitalization-based pension systems are sensitive to the ups and downs of prices of stocks, bonds and other financial instruments in the financial markets where pension funds are invested. Economic and financial volatility has been on the rise since the 1970s with the end of the Bretton Woods parities, the shift to flexible exchange rates, the oil price shocks of that decade and the overall deregulation and internationalization of financial markets worldwide. This inaugurated a long period of financial instability that features the Latin American debt crisis and the US Savings and Loan crisis in the United States in the 1980s, the crisis of the Exchange Rate Mechanism in Europe in the early 1990s, the East Asian and Russian crises of 1997–98, the Argentinean crisis of 2001, the Turkish 2002 crisis, and the global financial crisis of 2008–9 and more recently the extreme financial volatility of 2020 with the Covid-19 pandemic.[8] In particular, the global financial crisis of 2008–9 hit hard the value of pension funds in different economies that had privatized their pension systems such as Chile, Argentina, Poland, and Hungary. This is a fundamental weakness of pension systems based on individual accounts invested in capital markets. Some countries that privatized their pension systems tried to dampen this volatility by separating pension funds by return-risk combinations as the case of Chile since the early 2000s but without eradicating the impact of financial volatility on the value of pension funds.

---

[7] Besides the extent of the legal coverage of social security, other problem to ensure adequate pension levels is the *noncompliance* with social security taxes.

[8] Solimano (2020).

2.2 Historical Origins of Social Security and Pension Systems

2.2.1 Core Capitalist economies

As already mentioned, the first state-sponsored social security systems originated in Germany in the 1880s, promoted by the conservative chancellor Otto von Bismarck. In 1883, a health insurance system was created, followed by an accident insurance tier in 1884 and an old age and disability insurance in 1889.[9]

It is interesting to note that pension insurance, contrary to what occurs nowadays, was the least popular program. Life expectancy at that time was not very high (45–50 years); therefore, workers passed away shortly after retirement, making the subject of old age pensions somewhat less pressing.[10] The social security system was contribution-based, relying on payments from workers and employers (pay-as-you-go system) based on a social contract of intergenerational solidarity. The costs of mitigating social risks were borne mainly by the current generation. The Bismarckian system was occupational/tripartite rather than universal, relying on a system of tripartite financing. If the contributions exceeded the benefits, extra resources could be accumulated in a special fund. Nowadays, with a far larger life expectancy of the population, the convenience of having a reserve fund has acquired more importance.

In a broader context, the Bismarckian social security system was born to cope with the various social risks associated with rapid industrialization, displaced population from the countryside and lower-productivity jobs, in a process of structural transformations surrounded by insecurity, social activism and political tensions. The German system was later adopted by other European nations such as Denmark and the United Kingdom toward the end of the 19th century. After World War I, Italy and Spain in 1919, Belgium in 1924, Austria in 1928, France in 1930 and Portugal in 1935 also established their own social security schemes.

The efforts to create and promote social security at national level received a multilateral boost when in 1919, within the labor Committee of the Peace Conference in Paris, the International Labor Organization (ILO) was created by member states. Along with the promotion of better labor conditions, ILO promoted social security along the lines of the German model. Further, it adopted the principle of tripartite agreements (coordination and representation of workers, companies and the state). In 1927, the International Conference of National Unions of Mutual and Sickness Funds took place that turned into the International Association of Social Security (IASS). In 1944

---

[9] Eichengreen (2019).
[10] Bosch-Supan (2004), Voget (2008).

the Declaration of Philadelphia promoted a set of principles to guide comprehensive social security frameworks, based on international cooperation among institutions specialized in this area. In turn, the Philadelphia principles were incorporated in the Declaration of Human Rights in 1945, and later in the Convention of Economic, Social, and Cultural Rights of 1966.[11] On the other hand, the International Convention on Minimum Social Security Standards, summoned by the ILO in 1952, is still a relevant framework in this area.[12]

The United States adopted (rather late, compared to Europe) a *federal* social security system in the 1930s, motivated by the high social costs of the Great Depression (unemployment, income deprivation of families, loss of hope on the ability of capitalism to ensure good living standards to the working class and middle class) insufficiently protected by existing local and state institutions. Under the leadership of President Franklin D. Roosevelt, the US Congress approved the Social Security Act of 1935, creating a new federal system (which was not universal, but that could be expanded).[13] This scheme complemented other New Deal Programs of job creation and income support, aimed at reducing poverty and protecting the unemployed. Roosevelt proclaimed that though families and small communities were important mechanisms of social protection, in modern and complex societies social security needs to be provided by the state.[14] Even though the 1935 Act did not cover all contingencies—in particular, disability and medical benefits—it did include a pension plan for old people (extended to widows, children under 18 years old and very old parent survivors). These benefits would be financed by a salaried contribution as well as by general taxes.[15] However, the Social Security Act of 1935 fell short of creating a national health system in the United States comparable to that of Canada and other European nations.

Reflecting the high political priority of the Act of 1935, a directory of social security was created, reporting directly to President Roosevelt. There was also a massive effort to register the information of contributors and beneficiaries in order to administer payments properly. In 1946, the Directory of Social Security

---

[11] See Rodgers, Lee, Swepton and Van Daele (2009).

[12] See Chichon (2004).

[13] In the first decades of the 20th century, statewide pension and social protection plans existed in the United States, but these delivered generally modest benefits, with demanding criteria on eligibility.

[14] Early on, in 1912, President Theodore Roosevelt, directing himself to the Progressive Party of the United States, also stressed the need to protect citizens from unemployment, economic cycles, war, labor accidents, old age and other contingencies.

[15] Two programs (one state and the other federal) aimed at old age were created. The retirement age for men was set at 65 years, and the first pensions began to be regularly paid from 1940 (between 1937 and 1940 only onetime payments were made).

was substituted by the Social Security Administration (SSA), which is still in place today. An interesting peculiarity about the SSA is that it issues a "social security number" that is used as national identification cards, which is indicative of the importance and large coverage of social security in the United States.[16]

In the United Kingdom, as World War II was proceeding but peace loomed close, there was a need to ensure broad social protection to the population. In addition, the memories of the social hardship brought about by the depression of the 1930s were still very present. For that purpose, a set of institutions of social protection were created (or the existing ones strengthened), under the heading of the "welfare state." The main objective of the welfare state was to ensure the population's universal access to social security, health, education and housing once the war was over. This task was to be led by the Labor Party after its June 1945 general election victory over the Tories.[17] In 1940 Ernest Bevin, British Minister of Labor, commissioned the economist and politician Sir William Beveridge the preparation of a report to be presented to parliament outlining the main principles, concrete proposals and criteria of a comprehensive system of social insurance amenable of practical implementation. The report was published in 1942 under the title "Social Insurance and Allied Services," also known as the Beveridge Report, which turned into an inspiration and a guide for the operation of the postwar welfare state in Great Britain and to an extent it guided the creation of welfare states in other countries. This report proposed a social security system from "cradle to coffin" that would guarantee a basic standard of life applicable to all citizens, independent of their age, gender and occupational category. In turn, in 1944, Beveridge produced a second report entitled "Full Employment in a Free Society," arguing that effective social security also required full employment of the labor force. Beveridge shared similar ideas with John Maynard Keynes who was active in domestic policy advice in Britain and also the leading voice of the United Kingdom in the Bretton Woods Conference of 1944. On the other hand, Keynes also excelled as a theoretician when he published the *General Theory of Interest, Income and Employment*[18] that justified active state intervention to keep everybody at work in a volatile capitalist system.

---

[16] In the 1950s pensions began to be readjusted for inflation and by 1975 (Law of 1972) the readjustment COLA (cost of living allowances) became automatic. In 1954, the Disability Insurance Act was approved, and in 1965 (under President Lyndon B. Johnson) Medicare was created, which extended medical insurance to all citizens over 65 years old.

[17] In Europe, after World War II, social security benefits (such as old age pensions) were extended to employees and farmers. This was the case in France during 1946 and in Italy between 1957 and 1961.

[18] Keynes, (1936).

In 1946, the National Insurance Act was established, creating a comprehensive unemployment, sickness, maternity and old age pension system. At the same time, the NHS (National Health Service) was created, providing free-of-charge diagnosis and illness treatment in homes and hospitals. The Beveridge model was *universalist*, and the state assumed the administrative and financial responsibility to guarantee economic security for its citizens revolving around two axes: (i) full employment at the macroeconomic level, and (ii) social protection based on the ruling of both economic and social rights for everyone.

This two-pillar (macro-social) public policy prevailed in Britain for around thirty years after World War II. It was roughly endorsed by *both* conservative and labor governments during that period. The expansion of social security benefits in Britain and other European countries continued in the 1950s and 1960s with the postwar boom, but it was interrupted in the 1970s at the time of the oil shocks and the appearance of "stagflation" (a combination of inflation and stagnation) and other structural difficulties affecting the British economy. It is interesting that the initial reaction by several European governments to the difficulties of the 1970s was to *expand* social security benefits—encouraging, for example, early retirement for those who could not find a job—in order to mitigate the adverse shocks of the rise in unemployment.

2.2.2 Containment of social security benefits in the 1980s

The economic difficulties (slow growth, currency instability, inflation) and political problems of the 1970s (resignation of US president Richard Nixon in 1974, the Vietnam War, oil embargo and hostage crisis in Iran, labor strikes and terrorism in Europe) led to the questioning of how feasible it was to continue the expansion of social benefits in advanced capitalist countries. In the United Kingdom, economic turbulences and political unrest in the 1970s were expressed in growing civil discontent, union activism and strikes. In 1976, the unthinkable happened for a former imperial nation and the British government formally requested an emergency loan from the International Monetary Fund with its ensuing policy conditionality.[19]

In this context, the social-democrat-Keynesian postwar consensus that had dominated British economic and social policy begins to crack. A neoliberal anti–welfare state movement inspired on the ideas of Friedrich Hayek and Milton Friedman start gaining currency, inspiring Margaret Thatcher's platform for restructuring the British economy and its social institutions along neoliberal lines. She wins the general elections of 1979, and although she

---

[19] See Solimano (2017).

started a program of privatization of public enterprises and deregulation, social security was *not* fully privatized even though some individual capitalization schemes were introduced.[20]

A similar movement against Keynesian stabilization and the expansion of welfare benefits took place in the United States, during the 1980s under the government of Republican Ronald Reagan, who moved to curtail social security benefits, including Medicare, introducing a tax on pensions and cutting other social protection benefits.

2.2.3 *Further cuts in pension benefits during the 1990s and 2000s*

The tendency to *reduce* social security benefits was intensified in the 1990s and 2000s not only in the United States but also in continental Europe and even in Nordic countries. Benefits adjustment included:

(a) increase in the retirement age (reverting early-retirement policies) and containment of eligible beneficiaries for old age and disability pensions;

(b) changes in inflation-adjustment criteria applicable to pensions (de-indexation);

(c) changes in defined benefits (for instance, regarding prefixed replacement rates) to a system of defined contributions adjusted to general economic conditions;

(d) changes in the minimal number of years to be eligible for pensions (e.g., in France, the number of contribution years was raised substantially to be entitled to receive a pension); and

(e) introduction of complementary pension schemes based on individual accounts.

The winds of change in social security also reached Sweden that, as mentioned, launched a sophisticated system of "notional accounts" (see Box 2.1) in the mid-1990s trying to marry a pay-as-you-go system with the logic of individual capitalization. These reforms were approved by the Swedish parliament in 1994 and presented to the population as an adaptation of social security benefits to a less favorable labor market environment affected by slower growth in wages and employment along with changes in demography (increased life expectancy). Sweden's reforms included the creation of an individual account pillar that was managed by the state but in which a large number of private companies compete by offering investment alternatives to pension

---

[20] A similar approach for reforming pension systems was adopted in Australia and Sweden.

funds. The new pension model combined centralized administration of the pension system by a state agency (the Pension Contributions Authority, PCA), with a decentralization pattern of investment of pension funds.[21] Investments are decided by the contributor, but the agent that hires private fund management companies is the Swedish state.[22] This mechanism was preferred over the direct investment made by individual contributors, for two main reasons: (a) to exploit economies of scale in the collection of contributions, accountability, and information, which reduces the significant administration costs—which happens in countries that maintain private pillar of capitalization (as occurs in Chile, Australia, the United Kingdom and others) and (b) to guarantee an adequate supervision and regulation by the state of the private intermediators of pension funds.[23] The Swedish pension reforms were different from the privatization wave followed by Latin American and Central and Eastern countries in the 1990s and 2000s (see Chapter 3) not only in the introduction of notional accounts but also in the fact that the state retained an important guiding and regulatory role in the social security system.

In the United States, under President Clinton (1996–1999), new legislative changes were introduced to social security. These changes were aimed at *reducing* certain social benefits, making them more difficult to obtain. In particular, the Disability Act was modified, reducing eligibility criteria benefiting nonresidents (people without "Green Cards" or permanent residency permits); benefits accruing to alcoholics and drug addicts were also cut.[24]

In the United States, a small group started to push for considering the privatization of the pension system in the 1990s. This group was backed by some academics such as Harvard professor Martin Feldstein, formerly head of the Council of Economic Advisors in the first presidency of Ronald Reagan,

---

[21] See Palmer (2003). In the notional account model, contributions made from 1960 began to be registered as bonds in an individual account, to determine the "accumulated pension wealth" in a notional way. The annuity pension is calculated using an interest rate determined by the pension fund complemented with a (unisex) calculation of life expectancy. That way, the benefit of an old age pension is conceptually equivalent to the pension of a capitalization system based on individual accounts, although without actual monetary balances as accounts are merely notional.

[22] The period of saving accumulation (active working life) was separated from the insurance stage (retirement). The PCA acts as a public agency intermediating between contributors (individual accounts) and pension fund managers. The PCA relies on the National Tax Authority to collect contributions, the National Debt Office to invest funds, and the National Social Security Board for the transmission of information to contributors and local social security offices.

[23] In Sweden, workers and employees are also covered by collective insurances. These insurance policies are negotiated by the labor unions.

[24] Already in the 1980s there was an increase in verifications to permit disability benefits.

along with financial sector actors that entertained the prospect of handsome profits from intermediating a large pool of funds if individual funds were introduced as a mandatory system. In the early 2000s, Republican president George W. Bush proposed the creation of individual savings pension accounts offered to young workers but at the end full privatization of social security did not fly. Independent studies showed that the fiscal costs of turning social security into a private individual account scheme were significant, and that better pensions were not ensured even in a context of higher interest rates.[25] After the 2008–9 financial crisis, the privatizing impulse of social security of the early 2000s virtually vanished in the United States.[26] Later on, President Obama looked to strengthen public social security and increased budgets to improve operational procedures and the computational capacities of the SSA. He also approved an economic recovery bonus of US$ 250 paid only once to eligible adults in order to mitigate the costs of the 2008–9 crisis.

In several European countries reforms were made to their pension systems by changing benefit rules and introducing systems of funded individual accounts. However, these reforms stop short of dismantling the existing, dominant, public pillars. In 2003, France introduced two voluntary savings systems for old age: the PERP (Plan d' eparnage retraite populaire) and PEPCO (Plan d'eparnage de retraite collective). In 2014 the French parliament increased the number of years for contributions from 41.5 to 43, completing this adjustment in 2035, raising the effective age of retirement (currently at 62 years old).[27], [28]

Italy, in recent decades, also introduced changes to its social security system originally structured around the Bismarckian model. Reforms were motivated by high pension outlay ratios (close to 15 percent of GDP) along with the need to consolidate and unify rules and procedures in a country with around fifty different pension schemes. We can highlight the 1992–3 reforms (under the direction of Prime Minister Amato), the Dini reforms of 1995, the Prodi reforms of 1997, Maroni-Tremontini reforms of 2003–4 and the 2006–7 reforms of Prodi II.[29] The Dini reforms introduced a three-pillar system: (i) a

---

[25] See Geanakoplos, Mitchell and Zeldes (1998), Mitchell and Zeldes (1996), Kotlikoff (1998).

[26] See Diamond and Orzag (2005).

[27] For a person born in 1973 who entered the workforce at 23 years old, the effective age for retirement, in order to receive a complete pension after 43 years of contributions, would be 66 years old, even if the rule comes into effect in 2035. The new law also states that 50 percent of the obligations of the defined pillar system must have a backup fund.

[28] The contribution periods in the United Kingdom are 30 years, 38.5 years in Spain, and 40 years in Italy (c. 2012).

[29] See Guardiancich (2010).

public pillar including a notional accounts scheme of the sort implemented by Sweden in 1994. (ii) a semi-voluntary pillar offering complementary pensions and (iii) a nonmandatory pillar of individual accounts.[30]

Germany, the birthplace of the Bismarckian model, has also made reforms to its social security model. In 1992, it approved the Pension Reform Act, which changed indexation mechanisms and introduced stricter eligibility criteria for the unemployed and disabled. In 1996 the incentives for early retirement were reduced and adjustments to pension values based on life expectancy were modified in 1999. In 2001, the "Riester Reforms" were put in place (after the Labor Minister, Walter Riester), which reduced target replacement rates from 70 percent to 64 percent toward 2030. In addition, voluntary pension funds based on individual accounts have been created in recent years.

We have seen that changes to social security systems in advanced Western economies have usually focused on strengthening financial sustainability and containing pension and other benefits in light of demographic changes, labor market developments and increased fiscal costs. Nonetheless, we must reiterate that mature capitalist countries have avoided the sort of radical social security privatization as a fix to their social security challenges, the route adopted by various Latin American or Eastern/Central European countries in the 1980s (Chile), 1990s and 2000s although then reversed in several countries.

---

[30] The *first pillar*, public, has two subcomponents. The first component ensures a basic social pension to all the residents in Italy with at least 65 years of age, regardless of their history of contributions. The second component corresponds to a compulsory system of distribution that includes old age pension, disability and survival pensions with proportional benefits to the income of the workers. The quotation rate in this pillar is 32.7 percent for private sector employees (employer 23.8 percent and employee 8.9 percent) and 32.9 percent for public sector employees (24.2 percent for the employer and 8.7 percent for the employee); the (theoretical) replacement rate was of 78.9 percent in this pillar during 2005. The *second pillar*, semi-voluntary, of complementary pensions is based on funded accounts and includes tax incentives. A (major) part is administered by social entities, and another, negotiated collectively, by financial institutions. Finally, there is a *third pillar*, which has a voluntary character to its complementary pensions and includes two components: the first is called the Piano Individuale Pensiónistico (PIP) and another with open funds to individual affiliation. Both plans are administered by financial institutions, have defined contributions and contain tax advantages equal to those of the second pillar. Italy's social security administration is in the hands of the INPS (Instituto Nazionale per la Previdenza Sociale) for the private and independent sector and the INPDAP (Instituto Nazionale di Prevedenza per i Dipendenti dell'Amministrazione Pubblica) for public sector pensions.

2.3 Brief Historical Background of Social Security in Latin America

In Latin America, the mechanisms of social protection during the colonial era, to the extent they existed, followed the practices of the Spanish crown. The dominant modalities of social protection were administered by charitable organizations, guilds, the church and societies of mutual help. Entitlements to benefits by the population were directly related to their social and occupational status in the economy and society. Delegates from the Spanish royalty, director general, local administrators, landowners, and church dignitaries enjoyed more generous benefits than mid-level state employees, merchants, workers and peasants.

The Latin American *cajas* of the post-independence period (say the saving boards oriented to cover the costs of illness, accidents, survivors' pensions) come from the period of Spanish rule. The *montepíos* (allocations for retirement pensions and health costs) were created in the 17th and 18th centuries. They typically benefited army members and high-ranking civil servants, although over time these benefits also reached less privileged groups.

The Latin American experience in the 20th century with social security differs in important ways from the European and US experiences reviewed before. Social insurance schemes were more piecemeal and fragmentary rather than centralized and systematic. They benefited, first, organized pressure groups such as the army, railway workers, merchant marine, civil servants, parliamentarians and the so-called labor aristocracy (better-paid workers laboring in copper, gold and other high-value sectors).[31] Pension boards for different occupational groups did not have uniform rules, across the board: they differed in their levels of benefits, degree of social participation, financing methods, eligibility criteria, administrative modalities and legal structures. The modalities of organizing social security in Latin America, differed from the Bismarckian and Beveridge social insurance models that were designed in a centralized way at national level by central governments with more or less uniform rules across occupations in a less socially stratified way.

Social security institutions in Latin America developed first in the 1920s in countries with relatively more advanced development levels in the region. This was the case of Argentina, Brazil, Chile, Cuba and Uruguay. The emerging

---

[31] Authors such as Mesa-Lago have developed pressure group theories explaining the development of social security bodies in Latin America.

social security institutions addressed the social demands of working-class organizations and grassroots social movements along with the views of the authorities and their own models, motivated by the European experience. The influence of the very progressive Mexican constitution of 1917, drafted after the revolution of 1910, provided an advanced model based on social rights to education, health, labor legislation and pension systems. The recently created International Labor Office was also important in shaping new labor and social security legislation adopted in the 1920s in Latin America. A second wave of social security programs and institutions took place in the 1940s and the 1950s in Mexico, Venezuela, Peru, Columbia and Ecuador. Less developed countries such as Bolivia, Paraguay, Nicaragua, and Honduras adopted social security legislation in a later stage.

The financing methods of social security also showed considerable variation across programs and countries. Some programs received additional fiscal transfers financed through specific taxes, complementing contributions from workers, employees and employers. The degree of coverage of social benefits is positively correlated with variables such as the per capita income of the country, degree of urbanization and industrialization and government resources devoted to social protection. Latin American states followed a development strategy of import substitution industrialization (ISI) between the 1940s and the 1980s to switch to free market economics in the 1990s. In the developmentalist stage the productive, regulatory and social roles of the state were expanded but they fell short of European type of comprehensive welfare state. That state required taxation levels that local economic elites resisted to provide. The prevailing sociopolitical equilibrium with strong economic elites yielded only a moderate to low level of taxation that made a really protective and redistributive welfare state very difficult to finance. The tax base was always porous to the influence of specific interest groups that led to an increasing reliance on indirect taxes and natural resource taxation. Overall tax collection was further undermined by the existence of a large informal sector in several countries of the Latin American region.

The social security system that evolved between the 1920s and the 1970s through representing important social progress also accumulated a series of administrative and financial problems. Most pension systems were affected by chronic inflation due to the lack of indexation rules for benefits, a changing demography heading toward lower fertility rates and increase in life expectancy, social pressures for more benefits, actuarial deficits, lack of universality and homogeneity in functioning rules. A neoliberal response to these structural difficulties was the privatization of social security, the subject of the next chapter.

Chapter 3

THE RISE AND FALL OF PENSION PRIVATIZATION IN LATIN AMERICA AND CENTRAL AND EASTERN EUROPE

3.1 Introduction

A group of nearly thirty countries in Latin America and Eastern Europe launched ambitious programs of privatization of their pension systems in the 1990s and 2000s.[1] At that time, they were very receptive to the recommendations of the Washington Consensus of market deregulation, privatization of state assets and external sector opening because several governments were in need of the loans from international financial institutions. Latin America was emerging from the "lost decade" of the 1980s that led to a severe slowdown in economic growth, high inflation, fiscal deficits, debt servicing problems, increased poverty and higher inequality. Governments were, apparently, lured by the Chilean model of a private capitalization system introduced in the early 1980s by the Pinochet regime. This restructuring was far more radical than the adjustment to social security adopted by mature capitalist economies in North America and Europe (reviewed in the previous chapter). Within the framework of pay-as-you-go systems, they have focused on "parametric reforms"— rather than wholesale restructuring—increasing the retirement age, adjusting benefits and introducing of voluntary pension pillars; nonetheless, the social contract on which social security systems was built was not eschewed.

In contrast, the privatization experiments in developing and post-socialist countries went much further and brought in the financial sector to transfer the pension funds of wage earners to the corporate sector enabling massive funding and eventually wealth reallocation to capital owners.

---

[1] The term "Eastern" and "Central Europe" includes the former Democratic Republic of Germany, the Visegard States (Poland, Hungary, Czech Republic and Slovakia), the Baltic States (Estonia, Latvia and Lithuania), Bulgaria, Romania and countries of the former Yugoslavia.

The creation of mandatory individual accounts was seen as way to inject new savings to the local capital market in the expectation that with more financing available this would reinvigorate capital formation and accelerate economic growth. On the other side of the Atlantic, Eastern European nations—after the fall of the Berlin Wall and the end of the Soviet Union—embarked on an uncharted transition from centrally planned socialism to deregulated capitalism.[2] Under these conditions, the privatization of social security was viewed by free market economists and the emerging financial industry as a way to develop internal capital markets (virtually inexistent under central planning) and provide investment financing for private firms. Issues of high administration costs, declining coverage of social security benefits, adequacy of pension benefits and new intermediation costs were either downplayed or just considered as of limited relevance when privatized pension systems were launched.

3.2 Privatization within Worldwide Dominance of Public Pension Systems

In spite of the wave of pension system privatization of the past two to three decades, pension systems managed by public sector agencies operating under defined benefits rules are still dominant around the world. A study conducted by the World Bank[3] using a taxonomy of various pillars for describing pension systems in a variety of countries shows that 151 countries (circa 2010–12, out of 193 countries) had "pillar 1," say, compulsory national pension systems managed by the public sector with defined benefits related to years of contributions. The number of countries in the public pillar 1 represents 78.2 percent of the cases (Figure 3.1), showing the clear dominance of public pension systems in the world. Then 32 countries, mostly concentrated in Latin America and Central and Eastern Europe, created "pillar 2" (compulsory pension scheme based on individual accounts and managed by private corporations) after the pension privatization wave we have just described. The number of countries with pillar 2 represents 16.5 percent of the sample (Figure 3.1). Finally, in 81 countries (42 percent of the sample), there is also a "pillar 0"—corresponding to a non-contributive scheme providing basic/minimum pensions to low-income groups.[4]

---

[2] For analysis on post-socialist transitions in Eastern and Central Europe in the 1990s, see Becker (2016) and Solimano (2020).

[3] Pallares-Millares et al. (2012).

[4] In the case of Chile this corresponds to the *Pilar Solidario*.

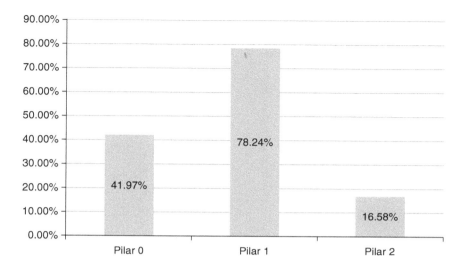

Figure 3.1. Percentage of countries in Pillars 0, 1 and 2 in the world (c. 2012)

Source: Own elaboration based on Pallares (2012).

3.3 The Cycle of Pension System Privatization and De-privatization

The international cycle of pension system restructuring of the late 20th and early 21st centuries in developing countries/emerging economies had two phases. First, a phase of *pension privatization* (partial or complete) in the 1980s–2000s that engaged 14 economies in Latin America, 14 countries in Central and Eastern Europe and Russia and two African economies: Ghana and Nigeria. Table 3.1 provides the dates of the privatization and then de-privatization for Latin American and Eastern European countries. As indicated before, no advanced capitalist country has so far privatized their social security system.[5]

The second phase of *de-privatization or re-reform* came after a decade or two of implementation of the privatization phase. In that sense the experiment was relatively short-lived for the typical life-cycle of a pension system. The exception, of course, has been the Chilean case, in which the system has been in place for nearly four decades. The re-reforms occur in at least 18 countries

---

[5] Holzman (2011) registers thirty cases of pillar 2 (individual accounts) creation between 1980 and 2008 (the majority located in Latin American countries and Central and Eastern Europe); while during that same period, Mesa-Lago (2014) counts 23 cases of capitalization pillar creation as part of a semi- or total social security privatization.

Table 3.1. Architecture of pension systems by regions of the world (c. 2012)

Region	Pillar 0	Pillar 1	Pillar 2	Number countries per region
East Asia and the Pacific	11	17	1	28
Eastern Europe and Central Asia	17	30	14	30
Latin America and Caribbean	19	29	10	37
Middle East and North Africa	2	18	1	20
South Asia	4	4	1	8
Africa sub-Sahara	8	33	2	46
High-income OECD countries	20	20	3	24
Total	81	151	32	193

Source: Pallares (2012).

out of the 30 privatizing/reformers.[6] This phase started in the early to mid-2000s in Venezuela, Ecuador and Nicaragua, with further reversals taking place since 2007 in Bulgaria, Argentina, Bolivia, Poland, Hungary, Russia, Rumania and Czech Republic.[7] The modalities of de-privatization included declaring unconstitutional the privatization of social security (Ecuador, Venezuela, Nicaragua, Bolivia), the downsizing of the private pillar and the closing down of the mandatory private accounts pillar (Argentina, Hungary, Poland). Let us first examine what was the logic and assumptions behind the privatization phase.

3.3.1 The privatization phase: Objectives, assumptions and reality

The project of privatization of pension systems had a set of (debatable) policy objectives and underlying economic assumptions regarding individual behavior, saving capacities, the nature of labor markets and financial markets that can be summarized as follows:

Overall Objectives

(A)   Promote individual savings by workers, employees and the self-employed as the chief mechanism to ensure economic security at old age. In practical terms, individual savings accounts are introduced into the social security system.

---

[6] Ortiz et al. (2018); Mesa-Lago (2014).
[7] See the study by the International Labor Office (ILO, 2018).

(B)   Replacement of the social contract based on principles of intergenerational solidarity and intrageneration redistribution on which the PAYG system is based for a logic of "individual responsibility" of savings to ensure, later at retirement age, a pension.

(C)   Promote the development of domestic capital markets to boost savings mobilization, raise financing for investment and support economic growth.

(D)   Reduce the burden of public social security on the fiscal deficit and public debt.

(E)   Increase financial choice in the preparation for retirement.

Underlying assumptions.

(F)   Individuals have a relevant saving capacity and are aware, at an early age, of the need to save for retirement (forward-looking mentality of economic agents, absence of myopia and low time-discount rates).

(G)   People have a significant understanding and knowledge of how financial markets in the real world behave. Individuals make rational/optimal choices balancing the risk and return profile of various financial instruments in which their pension funds are invested.

(H)   The fiscal costs of the transition from a pay-as-you-go system to individual accounts managed by private providers are small and transient.

(I)   The functioning of actual labor market in developing countries, characterized by informality, high job turnover, underemployment will not pose a main constraint for the proper operation of pension systems based on individual capitalization.

(J)   Capital markets do a fine job in allocating savings into the most profitable investment projects. The returns of investment are shared by the holders of individual accounts that will see their pension savings grow (geometrically) at a rapid rate over time yielding a nice pension at retirement.

Neglected issues and critical points.

It is apparent that the behavioral premises behind the capitalization model of pension reform rely on quite unrealistic assumptions of how a capitalist economy behaves in reality. These assumptions are particularly ill-suited for the reality of developing countries. The consequences of adopting reforms based on unrealistic assumptions can be summarized as follows:

(K) Overestimation of the savings capacity of low-income groups and large segments of the middle class in unequal societies in which labor earns modest wages.

(L) Reduced coverage of social security in economies with segmented and informal labor markets.

(M) Adverse impact on the level and volatility of pension savings invested in imperfect capital markets affected by segmentation, asymmetric information, market concentration, moral hazard and intrinsic complexity.

(N) Shift of the incidence of financial risks and longevity risks to holders of individual accounts.

(O) Regressive redistribution of savings from wage earners to large firms and big capital.

(P) Significant management and marketing costs of the pension funds industry.

(Q) The fiscal costs in the transition from a PAYG to a private capitalization system may last decades and be significant, running from around 3.6 percent of GDP in Argentina to 14.4 percent of GDP in Poland.[8]

(R) Governance issues in the private capitalization systems are reflected in the capture of regulators, implicit alliances between the pension management industry, policy makers and legislators and growing concentration in the pension fund management industry. The promise of more competition and de-politization of the pension system has not been fulfilled.[9]

(S) Lack of social participation and exclusion of workers and their organizations from the decision-making process of the pension management companies.

To avoid several of these problems there are a set of conventions and recommendations of the International Labor Office, ratified by national governments. However, in the privatization zeal, governments disregarded fundamental recommendations such as social dialogue and participation in the design of the pension system and its operation, balanced contributions between employers and employees, active role of the state in the provision of basic pensions, adequate pension levels, increasing coverage of social security and others.

The World Bank, after a strong endorsement of privatizing social security in the early to mid-1990s (see the *Averting Crisis at Old Age* Report), started to moderate its privatizing impetus after the arrival of Joseph Stiglitz as chief economist (later awarded a Nobel Prize in Economics) at the end of the decade. It became increasingly clear that the Old Age Crisis Report was based on very unrealistic assumptions like those listed above. Nowadays, the World Bank is

---

[8] ILO (2018).

[9] For internal (within the World Bank) but explicit criticism of the *Averting Crisis of the Old Age* report, see P. R. Orzag and J. E. Stiglitz (1999).

adopting a more balanced focus on pension reform, although still maintaining a pro–private sector stance emphasizing the creation of mandatory pillar 2 (individual accounts) for the elderly.

Before the 1980s, few people promoted an individual account pension system. The exception was Singapore but its scheme was managed through the

---

Box 3.1 Three modalities of pension privatization in Latin America*

(i) *"Substitute" reforms* in which the public pillar of distribution is closed: no new workers could enter to the PAYG pillar and must join, compulsorily, the private pillar of individual accounts. This case includes Chile (1981), Bolivia (1997), Mexico (1997) and El Salvador (1998).

(ii) *"Competitive pillar" reforms* in which the public pillar is maintained after the reforms that establish individual capitalization pillars and affiliates (e.g. new entrants to the work force) can choose between both options. This model was adopted in 1993 by Peru and by Colombia in 1994.

(iii) *"Complementary" or parallel pillar reforms* (mixed) in which the public pillar of pension is maintained—with certain adjustments—and a new individual account pillar is created. In this scheme people contribute to both pillars and can receive pensions payments from each during retirement. This was the case of Argentina (1994) and Uruguay (1996). The "substitute" model offered less choice for the affiliates to the pension system compared with the competitive and complementary modalities, as entrance to the public pillar was no longer allowed in the first option. In Chile, the public pillar (managing those who remained in the old *cajas*) became "residual" in the terminology of policy makers with its members dying over time. Only those who chose to remain in the old system could receive pension benefits (new entrants were barred from the old *cajas* administrative pillar). In contrast, the other two reform modalities allowed entry by workers to both pillars (public and private), either in a competing mode (modality ii) or in a complementary mode (modality iii). Anyhow, the incentives in the three cases were oriented to encourage contributors to choose the individual accounts pillar as a default option.

* See Mesa-Lago (1999).

Table 3.2. Full or partial privatization of pension system and reversals (de-privatization) in Latin America and Central/Eastern Europe

Latin America and the Caribbean		Eastern and Central Europe	
Privatization	**Reversion**	**Privatization**	**Reversion**
Chile (1981)		Hungary (1998)	2010
Peru (1993)		Poland (1999)	2013–14
Argentina (1994)	2008	Latvia (2001)	
Colombia (1994)		Bulgaria (2002)	
Uruguay (1996)		Croatia (2002)	
Bolivia (1997)	2009	Estonia (2002)	
Mexico (1997)		Lithuania (2004)	
El Salvador (1998)		Slovakia (2005)	2012
Nicaragua (2000)	2005	Macedonia (2006)	
Ecuador (2001)	2002	Romania (2008)	2017
Dominican Republic (2003)		Czech Republic (2013)	2016
Panama (2008)		Russia (2002)	2012

Source: Elaboration by the author based on E. Fulz (2012), C. Mesa-Lago (2014), K. Hijo and M. Kulli (2014), Ortiz et al. (2018).

state by a Central Provident Fund. The promoters of pension privatization and individual accounts rarely cite the case of Singapore in spite of being a system that has provided ample benefits to the population (pensions, health services, housing) due to the high savings rates of this country and the very professional way the Singaporean state has managed the system for over seven decades.

Although the wave of privatization of social security was supported by the OECD, USAID, InterAmerican Development Bank and the World Bank,[10] the position of the International Monetary Fund in the privatization drive was more guarded. In fact, the IMF recognized, early on, that establishing a pillar of individual accounts created a new source of fiscal imbalances. In fact, for several years the state has to continue serving the liabilities of paying pensions to retired individuals in the public pillar but contributions migrate to the individual account pillar. The ensuing fiscal gap (shortage of revenues over spending) alerted the IMF that this new reform could compromise "fiscal sustainability," a central concern in IMF's surveillance (every year IMF staff go to member countries to conduct evaluation of the macroeconomic situation and the possible appearance of imbalances in the fiscal budget and the balance

---

[10] See M. Pallares-Miralles, C. Romero and E. Whitehouse (2012) and Holzman, Hinz and Dorfman (2008).

of payments). Several studies commissioned by the IMF to explore the fiscal impact of pension system privatization confirmed these concerns.[11]

3.3.2 *The de-privatization phase: Reversals*

The global financial crisis of 2008–9 and the accumulation of fiscal deficits, dwindling coverage and meager pension benefits, high fees and commissions, capital market volatility, inequities in pension benefits across gender and socioeconomic groups were all features that prompted governments in Latin America and Eastern Europe to move away from privatized pension systems.

The extent of de-privatization and re-reform varied across countries. Some nations *terminated* the individual accounts pillar, in their mandatory modality; this was the case with Venezuela (2000), Ecuador (2002), Nicaragua (2005), Argentina (2008), Hungary (2010), Poland (2014), Russia (2012) and Czech Republic (2016). Other countries chose to *downsize* their pillars of individual accounts and return to public sector–managed pension systems that could ensure higher pension benefits and strengthen social rights rather than protecting profits of financial intermediaries. This was the case with Bulgaria (2007), Estonia (2009), Lithuania (2009), Latvia (2009), Macedonia (2011), Kazakhstan (2013), Croatia (2011), Slovakia (2013), Romania (2017). In the next section we examine in more detail the experience of Argentina, Poland and Hungary with de-privatization and re-reform of their pension systems.

3.4 The Pension Privatization/De-privatization Cycle in Argentina (1994–2008), Hungary (1998–2011) and Poland (1999–2014)

In 2008 Argentina ended the privatized pension system built around the AFJP (Administradoras de Fondos de Jubilaciones y Pensiones) and Hungary and Poland significantly reduced (termination) the size of their private pillars between 2010 and 2014, reverting privatization put in place by pro-business governments in the 1990s after the end of their socialist regimes. It is interesting to note that even in the privatization phase the three countries decided to *maintain* their public pillar financed by tripartite contributors. The private pillar in Argentina and Poland were managed by private for-profit companies, while in Hungary pension funds were intermediated by formally "non-profit entities".[12]

---

[11] See Heller 1998 and Barr, 2000.
[12] See Hirose, 2011.

3.4.1 *The case of Argentina*

The AFJP system in Argentina was launched in 1994 by President Carlos Menem, a Peronist president who had been incarcerated by the military regimes ruling his country between 1976 and 1983. However, once in power, Menem transformed himself into an active promotor of neoliberal policies and embraced the privatization of the pension system following closely the Chilean AFP model implemented a decade earlier. Nonetheless, there were some differences in the radicality of the privatization experiment: in Argentina at least one AFJP had to be state-run; in this case, the public AFJP was managed by the Banco de la Nacion and the ANSES (National Administrator of Social Security). In contrast, in Chile, no state-run AFP is allowed until today.

The social security system prevailing in Argentina before privatization extended benefits to a wide range of the population, although it also suffered various shortcomings: it runs chronic deficits due to insufficient contributions, evasion, informality, and increases in life expectancy. The privatization of the pension system in 1994 promised closing these financial deficits, while increasing the level of pensions to the population and enhancing choice in pension administration. All this would mobilize private savings, support investment and raise GDP growth.

The Integrated System of Pensions and Retirements (ISPR) that was created by Law 24.241 established a two-pillar system:[13]

(i)   A state-managed pillar that would deliver a Basic Universal Pension (BUP).
(ii)   A second pillar in which workers can choose between two regimes: a public pillar with defined benefits managed by ANSES and the individual capitalization, with defined contribution, managed by the AFJP. By default, a new worker getting a job had to enroll in an AFJP.

The new pension system increased the retirement age (60 years for women and 65 for men) and raised eligibility requirements to receive a pension from the public pillar from 20 to 30 years.[14] These measures reduced coverage and cut benefits. As people transferred their contributions to the new AFJP pillar and the state had to keep paying pensions to those in the ANSES (public pillar), a fiscal deficit developed. This deficit reached 3.3 percent of GDP in 2000, six years after the introduction of the new system.[15] To contain that deficit, state guarantees to pensions were reduced and the federal government

---

[13]   Cetrangolo and Grushka (2008).
[14]   Changes to the base of public benefits occurred to the person's three best yearly salaries, which led to a decrease in pensions. Cetrangolo and Grushka, 2008.
[15]   Cetrangolo and Grushka (2008).

absorbed the management of provincial *cajas*. In addition, the currency crisis at the end of the convertibility board in 2001–2 reduced the real value of pensions measured in Argentinean pesos.

To redress the decline in benefits of social security, President Nestor Kirchner introduced some important changes to the privatized pension scheme in the period 2005–7. A new pension law (26.222) was passed in 2007 that put a cap on commissions charged by the AFJP, expanded coverage and reduced the requirement that contributors had to pay for 30 years as an entitlement condition. It is estimated that after these measures social benefits expanded to 1.5 million people. Additionally, contributors were allowed, every five years, to choose between the PAYG and capitalization pillars. This led to nearly one million affiliates close to retirement age to return to the public pillar as their low accumulated balances in the AFJP's individual accounts render them to receive a meager pension.

Between October and December 2008, the private pillar was renationalized and a law on pension mobility (26.425) was passed that enabled the complete transfer of contributors from the private capitalization pillar (AFJP) to the public pillar managed by SIPA (Argentinean Integrated System of Pensions) within the ANSES. The AFJP ceased to exist as a compulsory scheme but they were given the choice of turning them into entities managing voluntary pension funds. The de-privatization process restored defined benefits: for a person contributing for 35 years, the replacement rate would be 75 percent of their last salaries. This was complemented by a noncontributory Universal Basic Pension. Outstanding balances deposited in the AFJP went to a Pension Reserve Fund created in 2007 to strengthen the financial sustainability of the pension system (the Guaranteed Sustainability Fund, GSF).[16] The GSF had assets representing close to 10 percent of GDP (2013). Some US$ 25 billion were transferred to the GSF and part of these funds were used to both close the fiscal gap (flows) and retire public debt (stock). In addition, the investment policy of the pension funds administered by the ANSES was modified and funds could no longer be invested abroad as under the AFJP system.

In retrospect, the AFJP experiment failed in Argentina for several reasons: (i) the fiscal imbalances created by the new system, which complicated macroeconomic management at a time the economy experienced the "convertibility crisis" of 2001–2 (crash of the one-to-one fixed parity between the Argentinean peso and the US dollar held in the previous ten years) and at the time of the global financial crisis of 2008–9, (ii) the lack of legitimacy of the private pillar among the public originated by the large fees charged by the AFJP, coexisting with modest pensions delivered by the

---

[16] Bertranou et al. (2011, 2018).

system (the capitalization pillar paid close to 450,000 pensioners during its existence). Once people were given freedom of de-affiliation from the AFJP, they massively returned to the ANSES (public pillar),[17] and (iii) the restoration of defined benefits formulas with explicit replacement rates and the commitment, backed by law, that the public system would honor the contributions made by the people to the AFJP encouraged rapid de-affiliation from the AFJP. Affiliates would receive a pension at least equal in value to the pension offered by the private pillar[18] The political economy of de-privatization in Argentina showed that the re-reform process had the broad support of the labor unions and the population at large. In turn, the backing of the AFJP comes mostly from a very debilitated financial sector.

3.4.2 The case of Hungary

During its socialist period, pension coverage in Hungary was almost universal. The system ruling since the end of World War II was framed along the lines of the Bismarckian model with contributions from the employees, the employers and the government. In the early 1990s a voluntary contribution private pillar of pensions was introduced along with a tripartite governing body and a poverty alleviation tier. In 1997 a complete restructuring of social security was undertaken along the lines of the privatized Argentinian system (rather than the Chilean one of the early 1980s) in which a PAYG pillar coexisted with a capitalization pillar (complementary systems, Box 3.1). The plan to privatize the pension system was negotiated with the trade unions and had the support of the socialist party, the World Bank and free market Hungarian economists. The new scheme introduced a four-pillar system:

(i)   Pillar 0 of basic pensions funded by social security contributions and general taxes.
(ii) Pillar 1, a mandatory public PAYG pillar with defined benefits financed by contributions from employers and employees.
(iii) Pillar 2, a mandatory private pillar, based on individual pension savings accounts managed by private entities.
(iv) Pillar 3, private, with voluntary contributions.

---

[17] With the de-privatization, those who were indecisive were sent to ANSES. This was the opposite of what happened in 1994; the indecisive were by default sent to the newly created AFJP.

[18] Página 12 (2008).

Since 1998, new entrants to the workforce by default had to go to the private pillar II. Individual accounts were intermediated by private (assumedly) nonprofit pension management entities, formed by associations of employers, chambers of commerce, trade unions, and voluntary pension funds, all joined in a cooperative model. Some of these entities were set up by commercial banks and insurance companies resembling more a commercial model. Pillar 2 invested the pension funds in government bonds, stocks, financial instruments offered by investment funds and other vehicles. The contribution rate from the employer to pillar 1 was initially set at 24 percent, although it was reduced to 18 percent for a few years. The contribution from employee to pillar 1 was initially set at 6 percent and then rose to 8 percent (until 2010). The retirement age increased, gradually from 1998 to 2009, from 60 to 62 years for men and from 55 to 62 for women.

Pensioners were expected to receive up to 75 percent of their pension from the public system and 25 percent from the private pillar. As of 2010 nearly three million people entered the mixed system representing over 70 percent of the labor force. The privatized pension pillar was advertised as leading to higher pensions, promote choice and efficiency with pension rights inherited (individual accounts were not offered by the public PAYG pillar). Despite the seemingly attractive features of the new system, at the end, the Hungarian private pension system experienced similar problems to those observed in other privatization experiments: a decline in pension benefits, an extra burden to the fiscal budget (in 2006 the fiscal deficit reached 9.7 percent of GDP) and high commissions and fees charged by pension management companies.[19] In addition, the real return for these investments was practically zero to even negative during the 12 years of implementation.[20]

Market concentration in the pension fund management industry was also significant. As of December 2010, while 18 financial entities managed the funds of the whole private capitalization pillar, only 5 of them concentrated 75 percent of its members and 82 percent of its assets. Replacement rates were modest: for the capitalization pillar, the rates were between 25 percent (with 20 years of contribution) and 50 percent (with 40 years of contribution).

---

[19] The total commissions for operation and management of assets as a percentage of value fluctuated between 2 percent (2000) and 1.45 percent (2009).

[20] In 2007, three funds were introduced (classic, balanced and growing), according to different combinations of profitability and risk. Hirose, 2011, Fulz, 2012.

Box 3.2 The Hungarian Parliament De-Privatization Act (November 2010)

In November 2010 the Hungarian parliament passed two Acts that opened the door to the de-privatization process:

(a) Act 100 enabling freedom of choice between remaining in the private capitalization pillar or returning to the public social security pillar.
(b) Act 101 that enabled a 14-month suspension, between November 2010 and December 2011, of the compulsory contribution to the private pension pillar, redirecting the contribution to the public pillar.

These two Acts were supplemented by Act 154 that regulated the transfer of assets from pillar 2 (individual accounts) to the recently created "Pension Reform and Debt Reduction Fund." This fund received nearly 10 percent of GDP in financial assets from the capitalization pillar and part of these funds were used to reduce the fiscal deficit (that turned to a surplus in 2011) and retire public debt. Contributors who returned to the PAYG public system (pillar 1) were recognized a *right to a complete pension* in exchange for the transfer of outstanding balances from the private pillar. Those who preferred to remain in the private system faced an increase in the contribution rate and rescinded the right of receiving a state pension.

As a result of these legal measures a massive return to the public pillar took place, with 97 percent of affiliates coming back to the public pillar (representing nearly three million affiliates). Only 3 percent of the affiliates decided to stay in pillar 2 (97,000 people).[a]

[a] Solimano (2017).

For the public pillar, they were higher: 33 percent with 20 years of contribution and 66 percent with 40 years of contribution.[21,22]

Like in the cases of Argentina and Poland, enlarged fiscal imbalances were one of the main reasons that led Hungary to de-privatizing the pension system

---

[21] Hirose (2011), Table 5.11.
[22] Up until 2008, 13 pensions per year were paid in Hungary. In October 2008, the country asked for an adjustment program entailing lending for more than $20 billion

(the EU and the IMF pressed Hungary to comply with European fiscal targets). In addition, the global financial crisis of 2008–9 had severe effects on the Hungarian economy with GDP falling by 9 percent in 2008–9. The conservative Fidesz government wanted to reduce its dependency on foreign creditors to finance the fiscal deficit and in 2010 Prime Minister Orban and the Minister of the Economy decided to end mandatory affiliation to pillar 2 and bring pension funds back to the public pillar. The nationalization of individual pension accounts, however, faced the opposition of the socialist party, the trade unions (although they were not fond of the presence of the pension private industry), the Green Party, some liberals and the association of private pension funds.

The re-reformed scheme after the changes of 2010–11 adopted defined benefits formulas (guaranteeing certain replacement rate for years of contribution), increased benefits for women, eliminated early retirement and compulsory retirement for civil servants, gradually increased the retirement age for men and women and removed disability payments from the pension system.

In retrospect, we may say that Hungary's privatization wave of the 1990s was somewhat less radical than the Chilean privatization of the early 1980s. Its design resembled more of the Argentinean system established in 1997. The PAYG defined benefits pillar was maintained although incentives encouraged new entrants to the labor market to go to the private pillar. During its 13 years of implementation (1998–2010), the system had a hard time to keep up with its promises of enhanced pension benefits, lower fiscal burdens, increased competition and more "consumer" financial choice. These problems led to a return to the public sector–managed pension system complemented by a voluntary pillar managed by national and international insurance companies. The renationalization phase, largely led by fiscal pressures, was somewhat complex in political terms as it faced the opposition of an unlikely alliance formed by several political parties, the trade unions and the lobby of the association of private pension management companies.

3.4.3 The case of Poland

The first social security reform in Poland in the post-socialist era took place in 1991. It was oriented to mitigate part of the social costs associated with policies of shock therapy that led to sharp initial drops in GDP, cut in real

---

from the IMF, European Union, and the World Bank. As an adjustment measure, the 13th month of pension was eliminated, along with increasing the retirement age from 62 to 67 years old, on top of a freeze on minimum pensions and changes in indexation rules.

wages and rising unemployment. Perhaps, surprisingly, these policies were adopted by the solidarity government of President Lech Walesa, whose origin was in the trade union movement. However, in retrospect, the initial slump in Poland was shorter than those experienced by other post-socialist transitions.[23] In 1999, the reform of social security went deeper into neoliberal lines and entailed the privatization of the pension system around a three-pillar system:

(i)   Pillar 1: A public PAYG pillar of defined benefits managed by the Social Security Institute (ZUS, according to its Polish initials). The total contribution rate was set at 19.52 percent (paid in equal parts by employers and employees) of which two-thirds went to the PAYG pillar (12.2 percent of gross wages).
(ii)   Pillar 2 of compulsory, private individual accounts with defined capitalization contributions. The pillar was to be managed by a private "open pension fund" (OFE in Polish). A third of the total contribution rate went to this pillar (7.3 percent of gross wages).
(iii) Pillar 3, voluntary pensions managed by several private pension funds.

The new system was promoted on various grounds: to foster closer links between contribution efforts and future pensions (logic of "individual responsibility"), enhanced financial choice and competition, reduced fiscal burdens and private savings mobilization. Nevertheless, the reality of lower wages and involuntary unemployment (Polish emigration to Western Europe has been significant during its post-socialist transition to capitalism), the high fees charged by the intermediation industry and the fiscal impact of the reforms were relevant factors largely overlooked in the quest for privatization of the pension system. The reforms of the late 1990s made political compromises, and special pension schemes funded from general tax revenues and contributions were preserved for certain occupational/pressure groups such as farmers, armed forces, national police, gendarmerie and the judiciary. In addition, a Demographic Reserve Fund was created.

The Polish pillars 1 and 2 were based on individual accounts according to defined contributions (DC) principles. In turn, the public pillar was based on notional balances growing at a theoretical/notional rate of return (based

---

[23] Lasek Balcerowicz, Minister of Finances, had an important role in the design and implementation of transition policies, assisted by international macroeconomic experts such as Jeffrey Sachs. The shock therapy program had the financial and technical support from the IMF and the World Bank and the support of the US government. Solimano, 2020.

Table 3.3. Average commissions charged by private pillar 2, percent (OFE)

Period	Commission
1999–March 2004	10%
April 2004–09	7%
2010–13	3.5%
2014–	1.4%

Commission asset management is 0.6% a year.

on the growth rate of wages and labor productivity, similar to the Swedish model), while the interest rate in pillar 2 was market-determined.

The evolution of average commissions/fees charged by private pension companies operating in Pillar 2 is presented in Table 3.3.

Even though commissions declined over time, they reached high levels (between 7 and 10 percent) for a period of 10 years (1999–2009), diminishing the net value of the pension funds and therefore reducing future pensions. Estimates by Oreziac (2016) are that close to $10 billion were paid in commissions by Polish affiliates to pension fund management companies between 1999 and July 2014, an important resource transfer from wage earners (hit hard by the post-socialist transition) to private pension companies.

In Poland, as in Hungary and Argentina, pension privatization created fiscal imbalances: it is estimated that the cumulative fiscal gap created by the shift to the private pillar in the period 1999–2012 was 14.4 percent of 2012 GDP.[24] In addition, the public pillar was also running a deficit largely for paying benefits larger than planned.

Oreziac (2016) estimates that the pension fund tier OFE accumulated US$ 96 billion in deposits until January 31, 2014, when privatization is reverted. These funds supported: (i) the process of capital accumulation in the capitalist sector of the economy, (ii) financed fiscal deficits, and (iii) exports of savings abroad. To reduce the fiscal cost of the reformed pension system, the Polish government eventually downsized sharply the private capitalization pillar and increased the retirement age.[25]

---

[24] A 6.6 percent of GDP corresponded to servicing additional public debt. Polakowsky and Hamejer (2018).

[25] From 60 to 66 years for women (the process should be completed in 2040) and from 65 to 67 years for men.

Nationalization of pillar II and other changes

In Poland, the de-legitimation of the capitalization system (high fees and low pensions) combined with an adverse fiscal situation led to the Pension Act on December 2013 that nationalized the OFE pillar (actively supported by the Ministry of Finance and the Ministry of Labor and Social Policy). The following specific policy measures were adopted, enacting various responses from affiliates:

(i)   Freedom of de-affiliation to the OFE. People could choose between returning to the ZUS (state pillar) or staying at the OFE (private pillar).
(ii) As a response to the freedom of de-affiliation, 55 percent of the financial balances in the individual accounts were transferred from OFE to ZUS (February 2014), with 45 percent of the balances remaining at the OFE pillar.
(iii) In a period of 10 years before the retirement age, one-tenth of the individual account's assets must be transferred to ZUS. The contributions from that period must go to ZUS.
(iv) Prohibition of the OFE to invest in government bonds.
(v)   Reduction of fees and commissions charged by the OFE.

As a consequence of these measures, out of a total of 16.5 million affiliates in the OFE in early 2014, 14 million (85 percent of the total) migrated to the ZUS public pillar and 2.5 million (15 percent) stayed in the private capitalization pillar. The migration of financial resources (accumulated balances) from the OFE to ZUS represented nearly 15 percent of Polish GDP. In general, beneficiaries with higher balances in their individual pension accounts tended to stay in the private pillar 2 and those with lower balances migrated to the ZUS. In fact, the 15 percent of the affiliates that stayed in the OFE had balances representing 48.5 percent of total balances in the private pillar.[26] The percentage of beneficiaries who transferred to the public pillar (ZUS) after de-privatization was lower in Poland than in Hungary: 85 percent versus 97 percent in the latter.

3.4.4 Lessons of comparative international experience in de-privatization

The review of the pension privatization and de-privatization cycles in Argentina, Hungary and Poland suggests several conclusions and common features:

---

[26] One can think of a Lorenz Curve relating the number of affiliates ordered by their balances in the individual accounts and the cumulative share of pension funds in those accounts.

a)   Initially, the privatization of pension regimes in the three countries was promoted as a solution to the preexisting difficulties in pay-as-you-go systems such as heterogeneity of rules, fragmentation, fiscal deficits, adverse effects of demography, lack of choice and inflationary erosion of the real value of pensions. However, in general, the promise of better pensions did not materialize and the experiments came accompanied by higher fiscal deficits, significant fees charged by pension management corporations, volatility in capital markets, reduced coverage and absence of workers' participation in the management of pension funds. All these problems ultimately undermined citizens' support to the privatized system and led governments to reduce or eliminate the compulsory private pillars, reversing pension privatization. When affiliates were given freedom of choice, they, massively, decided to transfer their funds to the public pillar, although still a small percentage of contributors (those with higher balances in their individual accounts) preferred to remain in the private pillar.

b)   The pension privatizing processes in the 1990s were often adopted with limited public discussion on the merits and costs of the proposed new system. Workers' organizations and independent observers had less influence than domestic and international financial institutions. This is in contrast with the conventions and recommendations coming from the International Labor Office stressing the need for "social dialogue" in pension reform. The ILO and other critical observers highlighted the risks of launching these privatizing reforms "from above" (led mainly by governments, their economic technocracy and the financial community) without due democratic consultation.

c)   Privatization of pension system was included in the policy *conditionality* of the World Bank, regional development banks and, in some cases, the IMF. The financial sector and big business associations generally supported this process.

d)   Unlike the case of Chile, the privatization reforms in Argentina, Hungary and Poland maintained, after the new system was in place, their public pillars active and secured contributions for that purpose.

e)   The experiments with privatized pension systems generated significant fiscal imbalances on the order of 3–5 percent of GDP in Argentina, Poland and Hungary in the transition period lasting several years or even decades. This was due to the combination of diminished contribution and outstanding pension commitments to the public pillars associated with the shift to capitalization.

f)   In the de-privatizing phase, governments abolished laws approved during the privatization phase requiring compulsory contributions to private pension management companies and decreed freedom of de-affiliation from the capitalization pillars. In Argentina, more than 90 percent of affiliates returned to the public system of pay-as-you go in Hungary 97 percent and in Poland that ratio was 85 percent. The volume of assets transferred to public reserve funds after de-affiliation from private pillars represented around 10–15 percent of GDP in the three countries.

g)   The transfer of balances from the individual accounts to public reserve funds was accompanied by commitments, supported by new laws, that guaranteed the state to pay pension benefits that were generally higher than the pensions paid in the private pillar.

h)   The de-privatization of social security in Argentina, Poland and Hungary was *not* accompanied by financial crises and macroeconomic instability that often entail declines in asset prices, depreciation of the national currency and larger *spreads* of public sector debt and private debt in international capital markets. On the contrary, external confidence was fortified as an important source of fiscal imbalances was reduced or eliminated.

i)   The population generally supported the de-privatization of the pension system as they were unsatisfied with a reality of low pensions, high fees and the prospects of higher taxes to cover privatization reform-induced fiscal imbalances.

j)   An important element that facilitated the de-privatization of pension systems in the three countries was the fact that they had in place universal/distributive public pension pillars during the privatization experiments, which provided organizational capital and important management capabilities to receive a return of a large contingent of affiliates coming from the private pillar.

Chapter 4

THE EVOLUTION OF SOCIAL PROTECTION AND PENSION SYSTEMS IN CHILE FROM THE 19TH CENTURY UNTIL ITS PRIVATIZATION IN THE 1980S

4.1 Introduction

This chapter presents a historic overview of the origins and evolution of social insurance, pension schemes and labor legislation in Chile since the mid-19th century until the privatization of the pension system in the early 1980s, during the Pinochet regime. The analysis seeks to place the evolution of social protection and pension systems in the broader context of the development strategies followed by the country in different periods of its history along with their corresponding political background. It is important to note that both in the colonial period and after independence, economic elites (national and foreign) have been very important as owners in mining, finance, industry and agriculture activities and have wielded very significant political and public policy influences.

Consequently, Chile is a country of deep structural inequalities of incomes, wealth, access to social services and political power. Nonetheless, this inequality and entrenched power structures have also been contested by mass movements and progressive political parties. In the early 20th century, Chile faced the eruption of an organized labor movement that sought to redress the most acute manifestations of poverty and social exclusion; this was the so-called *cuestión social*. Social protest and the influences of the Mexican Revolution (1910) and even the Russian Revolution (1917) conducted to a situation in which new social and labor legislation was adopted in Chile in the mid-1920s. In 1925 young army officers sensitive to the social situation of the masses pressed Congress and the political class, after a delay, to adopt progressive new laws.

The prevailing literature on social security in Latin America [1] stresses the influence of organized social groups and relatively powerful sectors in society such as the army and civil servants to secure for themselves social insurance and pension systems. In line with these theories in Chile, the military, the national police (*Carabineros*), civil servants, railway workers, merchant navy workers, employees of the banking system were also able to set up *cajas* (pension and health boards) with higher benefits than those received by manual workers (the *obreros*). Rural workers and the self-employed were often excluded from formal social security. However, pressure groups have success in pressing for their demands when the overall social situation features poverty, inequality and exclusion.

Historically, between the 1920s and 1973, Chile was considered as one of the regional leaders in the adoption of progressive social protection mechanisms. In fact, the two governments of Alessandri Palma one in the 1920s and the other in the 1930s, Pedro Aguirre-Cerda and the radical party presidents in the late 1930s and the 1940s, Carlos Ibanez del Campo in the early 1950s, Alessandri, Frei-Montalva in the 1960s and Allende in the early 1970s all tried some way or the other to expand the coverage of social security benefits to reach women, rural workers and small-scale owners, workers in the trade and transport sector and the self-employed. At the same time, there was more awareness on the need to introduce more homogeneity of rules across the *cajas*, ensure better social benefits, adopt price-indexation of monetary payments and strengthen financial sustainability of the pension boards with varying degrees of success (and failure). Social security funding was based on tripartite contributions and combined pay-as-you-go and capitalization funding mechanisms. [2]

The military regime that emerged from the coup of September 11, 1973, also sought to reform social security but was unclear in which way to go. As discussed in Chapter 1, from 1973 to 1979, corporatist views supported by the air force competed with a free market orthodoxy represented by the economist trained at the University of Chicago and Harvard University that were gaining increasing influence in the design of labor and social policy of the military dictatorship and convinced Pinochet of the privatization of the pension system.

4.2 Development of Social Security and Labor Legislation from the 19th Century

In the 19th century the provision of social insurance was organized by the church, labor unions, and mutual help societies. In 1832 a public charity and

---

[1] Mesa-Lago, 1978
[2] Arellano, (1985).

health board was established, followed by a law of military *Montepio* granting survivors pensions for widows and orphans of army members, in 1855. Then, in 1858, the Caja de Ahorros de los Empleados Públicos (Savings Board for Public Employees) was created.

In the second half of the 19th century, few new labor laws were passed. However, this changed in the early decades of the 20th century coinciding with an increased degree of labor activism and social unrest, including strikes and protests, some of them bloodily repressed by the Chilean army as it was the case of the Santa Maria massacre of 1907 involving the death of thousands of nitrate workers and their family members in a school in the northern city of Iquique. A year early, in 1906, a housing law for low-income groups was passed that tried to improve the crowded living conditions affecting working-class families coming to cities from depressed mining areas (nitrate sector) in the north of the country. A Sunday holidays law was passed in 1907 that allowed workers to have one day of rest per week in industrial and commercial enterprises. This was followed by the child protection law of 1912. In 1914 a law was passed that required companies in the commerce sector to provide chairs for their employees to afford long work journeys. This was called the *ley de la silla*. Moreover, job accident legislation was passed in 1916, a nursery law in 1917 and a law regulating heavy work in 1923 (see Table A.1 in the Annex). Another influential occupational group, the workers and employees of the railway system that played a critical role in connecting different parts of the Chilean territory since the second half of the 19th century and early 20th century, managed to form a savings board in 1911, followed by the Caja de Ahorros de Empleados de Ferrocarriles del Estado established in 1918.[3]

The degree of enforcement of these various laws is not entirely clear but at least they represented the start of legally sanctioned social protection. An important institutional milestone was the creation of the "Oficina del Trabajo" (Labor Office), in 1907, dependent of the Ministry of Public Works. Initially intended to serve as a register of labor statistics, it also helped in the formulation of labor laws and performed roles of inspection and mediation of labor conflicts.[4] The Oficina del Trabajo evolved into the General Labor Directorate in 1924 and the Ministry of Hygiene, Assistance and Social Security in 1925. This, in turn, was transformed into the Ministry of Welfare in 1927 by the first government of Carlos Ibáñez del Campo and turned into the Ministry of Labor in 1932, the year of the short-lived Chilean "workers republic." Several decades later, in 1959, this ministry again mutated into the Ministry of Labor and Social Security, its current denomination.

---

[3] See Benavides and Jones (2012).
[4] Yáñez Andrade, (2008).

The first formal old age pension board, called the Caja de Retiro y Montepíos del Ejército y la Armada, was set up in 1915 for the army and navy. This *caja* was preceded by the Sociedad de Proteccion de Viudas y Huerfanos de Mártires de la Patria created in 1879 at the time of the Pacific war with Peru and Bolivia. The society provided assistance for disabled war veterans, their widows and orphans. Decades later, in 1953, under the second presidency of General Carlos Ibáñez del Campo (1952–58), the 1915 Pension Board for the Army was strengthened and renamed as the Caja de Prevision de la Defensa Nacional, CAPREDENA (its current denomination).

4.2.1 The Rush of Labor Legislation in the 1920s

In 1920, President Arturo Alessandri was selected around a platform of social and labor reforms. Several draft laws addressing demands for workers protection were presented in 1921 (some of them had been presented by the previous government in 1919), but their approval was stalled for three years in National Congress. It was only under the protest of army officers in September 1924— the *ruido de sables*—followed by the takeover of government by a military junta and the exile of President Alessandri, that the National Congress, in a rush, approved the pending bulk of socially oriented legislation.

The main new legislation approved in 1924 included:

(A) A new labor contract law establishing an eight-hour work limit per day, banning child labor and regulating women work. This law was, apparently, inspired by the recommendations of the International Labor Office.
(B) New legislation concerning prevention and compensation to the injured and their families in case of job accidents.
(C) A General Labor Directorate was commissioned to oversee the enforcement of labor and social security laws.
(D) A trade unions law.
(E) The creation of the Caja del Seguro Obrero Obligatorio (mandatory social insurance board for blue-collar, manual workers).
(F) The establishment of the Caja de Prevision de Empleados Particulares (Pension Board for Private Sector Employees).
(G) Creation of the Ministry of Hygiene, Social Assistance and Pensions.

In 1925 legislative changes in the political and labor fields included:

(H) A new constitution that replaced the charter of 1833, strengthening the powers of the president and leaving behind the parliamentarian regime in place since the end of the civil war of 1891. The new constitution of 1925 was also progressive in terms of granting new social rights to the population.

(I)   The creation of the Caja de Ahorro de Empleados Públicos y Periodistas (Pension Board for Public Sector Employees and Journalists).

(J)   Pension and Social Assistance Board for the fiscal and local police.

This last legislation deserves some comment. In 1927 (presidency of Carlos Ibañez del Campo), the existing bodies of fiscal, urban and rural police were unified and centralized with the creation of Carabineros de Chile. In addition, it created DIPRECA, the pension system of Carabineros de Chile.[5]

In the 1930s and the 1940s, new *cajas* (pensions boards) were created for employees of the merchant navy (1937), racetracks (*hipódromos*, 1941) and commercial banks and credit institutions (1946); see Table A.4.1. Previously, a Popular Housing Fund was created in 1936 and health services expanded (Preventive Health Law of 1938). Several of these laws were approved in the second government of Arturo Alessandri Palma (1933–38).

The funding mechanisms of the different *cajas* followed, in general, the Bismarckian tradition of compulsory contributions by employers and employees and in some cases with the government providing additional funding, as in the case of the Caja de Seguro Obrero. Some *cajas* used pay-as-you-go funding for covering health expenses and the liabilities of occupational risks (work accidents, unemployment, disability) with capitalization (investment of accumulated contributions) financing old age pensions.[6]

The decision-making process of the *cajas* was, in general, participatory and based on councils constituted by representatives from workers, employers, and the state. In a sense, they were "quasi-public institutions." Accompanying these reforms there was a, increase in overall social spending (see Box 4.1 and Table 4.1).

During most of the 20th century, the labor legislation and the pension schemes made a sharp class distinction between manual workers (blue collar)

---

[5] In his first government, 1927–31, Carlos Ibañez del Campo ruled as an authoritarian leader. However, his government became rapidly debilitated with the economic crisis of the early 1930s that hit Chile badly; in fact, the League of Nations declared that Chile was the worst-affected country by the Great Depression (see Solimano, 2020). In mid-1931, Ibañez resigned from the presidency and sought asylum in Argentina but decades later won the presidential elections of 1952 and returned to the presidency.

[6] Members could choose the "cash option" and withdraw their accumulated funds once they reach retirement age with the majority doing so (Arellano, 1985, 75). The Caja de Empleados Particulares (for employees in the private sector) for old age pension relied only on contributions from employers and employees. The Caja de Empleados Públicos y Periodistas (for public sector employees and journalists) established an old age pension after 40 years of service and 65 years of age.

and clerical and professional employees (white collar). The benefits of the first group were lower than the benefits of the second segment, contributing to the fragmentation of the pension system in which different *cajas* had different eligibility rules, contribution rates and benefits.[7]

Chile led regional initiatives to improve social protection. In 1942 it convened the first Inter-American Social Security Conference at a governmental level. Salvador Allende, at time the Minister of Public Health and Social Security of President Pedro Aguirre Cerda (1938–41), played an important role in the organization and the steering of this regional meeting.[8]

4.2.2 The Reforms of 1952–53

In the 1950s, important reforms of the pension and health systems took place that were initiated in the previous decades. The era of *presidentes radicales*, center-left, 1938–52 (Pedro Aguirre-Cerda, Juan Antonio Rios and Gabriel Gonzalez-Videla), was followed by the second government of Carlos Ibanez del Campo of a centrist-populist bent (1952–58). Then, it came the conservative government of Jorge Alessandri Rodriguez (1958–62). Notwithstanding their ideological differences, there was an implicit consensus on the importance of expanding social security benefits while ordering a system of increasing heterogeneity.

The reforms of the early 1950s included the creation of the Servicio de Seguro Social (SSS) that reorganized the Caja de Seguro Obrero operating under a defined benefits modality. Another innovation was the creation of the Servicio Nacional de Salud (SNS), a National Health Service, that centralized the provision of health services, somewhat in the way of the British health system created by the Beveridge plan. The SNS extended health services to family members of the contributors. Some of the reforms included the Caja de Empleados Particulares (EMPART) y la Caja de Empleados Públicos y Periodistas (CANAEMPU), operating under defined benefits rules. In the case of public employees, the age of retirement was set at 65 for men and 60 for women.

The reforms of 1952–53 were an improvement over the systems of the 1930s and the 1940s, but still some important problems remained to be tackled. They referred to: (a) securing the real (inflation-adjusted) value of pension benefits, (b) extending benefits coverage to women, (c) extending the reach of the social security system to rural workers, the self-employed and

---

[7] Arellano, (1985).
[8] See Rodgers et al. (2009).

marginalized urban workforce, (d) reducing the heterogeneity of rules across subsystems, (e) reducing the operational and financial complexity of the *cajas*.

These concerns were examined in the report of the Klein-Sacks mission (a team of private economic advisors hired by the Ibanez government to help stabilize inflation).[9] Their diagnosis of the shortcomings of the pension boards focused on their heterogeneity in rules and benefits, the influence of pressure groups and financial sustainability problems. They recommended simplification of procedures and rules unification across *cajas* (Klein-Saks, 1958).

The conservative government of Jorge Alessandri (1958–64), son of former president Arturo Alessandri, appointed the "Prat Commission"[10] to make a diagnosis of the social security system and provide recommendations for reform. After several years of work, the commission produced a 500-page report, rich in detailed descriptions and suggestions for change, but the Alessandri government ended its term and no reform was passed by parliament.[11] The task was left for future governments.

4.2.3 Reform Efforts by the Frei-Montalva and Allende Governments

The Christian Democratic government of Eduardo Frei Montalva (1964–70) announced its intention to reform the pension system through the rationalization of existing *cajas* while expanding benefits to rural workers (peasants and temporary agricultural workers) and other marginalized groups in Chilean society. This connected well with agrarian reform and the law of peasant unionization that were important priorities of the Frei-Montalva government. However, a setback for the government plans was the rejection in Congress in 1969 of a draft law oriented to simplify and homogenize rules of the social security system.

The Allende government, of socialist orientation, also wanted the reform of the social security system through simplification, rule harmonization and financial sustainability, goals that were broadly shared by the three presidential candidates in the national election contest of 1970 (the candidates were Jorge Alessandri, Radomiro Tomic and Salvador Allende).

The Allende administration proposed an increase in the level and coverage of pension and health benefits for manual workers, the middle class and the

---

[9] This mission shared an approach to economic adjustment similar to the teams of the International Monetary Fund.

[10] The head of the commission was the lawyer Jorge Prat.

[11] Comisión de Estudios de la Seguridad Social, Chile (1965). *Informe sobre la reforma de la seguridad social chilena*, volume 2. Santiago: Editorial Jurídica de Chile.

Box 4.1 The Trend of Rising Social Spending

The statistical evidence suggests a rising trend in social spending in education, health, pensions and housing from the mid-1920s (starting at a very low level) through the early 1970s. We can distinguish three subperiods: (i) expansion from 1925 to 1955 in which the ratio of social spending increased from 2.5 percent of GDP in 1925 to 15 percent of GDP in 1955; (ii) a second period of consolidation between 1955 and 1972, with social spending reaching a peak of 26 percent in 1972, during the Allende government; and (iii) a third period, between 1973 and 1983 (Pinochet regime) of retrenchment of social spending in which the social spending ratio to GDP declines to a low of 14 percent in 1981. A similar trend is experienced by the level of spending in pensions (as shares of total social spending and GDP). Pension spending increased steadily between 1955 and 1972–73 and declined thereafter (see Figure 4.1 and Table 4.1).[a] Outlays on old age pensions, disability and family allowances increased from 6.1 percent of the GDP in 1955 to 11.5 percent in 1972 to then diminish to 8 percent in 1983.

[a] Numbers from J. P. Arellano, *Políticas Sociales y Desarrollo: Chile, 1924–1984* (Santiago: CIEPLAN, 1985).

---

armed forces. The level of minimum pensions was to converge to the minimum wage with funding coming from progressive direct taxation. Although Allende did not receive congressional support to pass a complete overhaul of the pension system with expanded benefits, in 1972 his government managed to create a new pension regime for merchants, small- and middle-sized enterprises, the self-employed and the transport sector.

Another feature of the Chilean pension system was the differences in benefits across occupational groups. A traditionally privileged position in terms of social security benefits was enjoyed by the armed forces and national police; probably every government wanted to have those enjoying the monopoly of arms and weapons satisfied. This traditional gap between pensions paid in the defense sector relative to the civilian population (see Table 4.2) accentuated after the military coup of September 1973 (see Chapter 5).

Table 4.1. Chile: Social Spending 1935–83

Year	Social Expending		Components of Social Spending							
	billions $1981	% of GDP	Public Health, Social Help and Employment	Pension Benefits	Housing and Urban Planning	Education	Public Health, Social Help and Employment	Pension Benefits	Housing and Urban Planning	Education
			% of Social Spending				% of GDP			
1925	3,1	2,1								
1935	12,3	5,2								
1945	23,3	8,0								
1955	55,1	14,9	17,9	41,4	20,4	20,3	2,7	6,2	3,0	3,0
1961	85,4	17,0	18,9	51,4	11,5	18,1	3,2	8,7	1,9	3,1
1963	90,4	16,3	20,1	46,6	15,1	18,2	3,3	7,6	2,5	2,9
1965	124,2	20,0	18,0	45,5	17,9	18,6	3,6	9,1	3,6	3,7
1967	159,5	20,1	15,7	46,0	17,8	20,6	3,2	9,3	3,6	4,1
1969	180,8	18,7	16,2	43,6	17,8	22,4	3,0	8,2	3,3	4,2
1970	206,9	19,9	16,4	45,2	16,0	22,4	3,3	8,9	3,2	4,5
1971	274,4	25,2	15,8	45,9	16,3	21,9	4,0	11,6	4,1	5,5
1972	226,2	25,8	16,8	44,4	15,9	23,0	4,3	11,5	4,1	5,9
1974	182,6	17,6	16,2	36,6	21,5	25,7	2,9	6,4	3,8	4,5
1975	153,2	18,3	18,0	41,9	15,7	24,4	3,3	7,7	2,9	4,5
1977	165,8	17,4	20,3	40,4	13,4	25,9	3,5	7,0	2,3	4,5
1979	191,7	15,4	19,4	44,2	9,9	26,6	2,9	6,8	1,5	4,1
1981	202,1	14,3	21,8	43,4	9,4	25,3	3,1	6,2	1,3	3,6
1983	206,1	17,1	24,6	47,1	5,3	23,0	4,2	8,1	0,9	3,9

Table 4.2. Pension as a Percentage of the Average Pension for the Country, 1965–80 (average = 100)

Year	Private Sector Workers (blue collar)	Private Sector Employees (white collar)	Civilian Public Sector Employees (white collar)	Armed Forces and National Police (Carabineros)
1965	49	128	90	203
1969	52	131	170	212
1970	49	116	168	245
1971	50	94	153	293
1972	52	94	130	338
1973	57	67	127	346
1974	51	68	146	361
1975	53	77	157	283
1976	54	75	152	334
1977	53	77	131	370
1978	56	74	131	335
1979	49	88	150	332
1980	46	77	148	350

Source: Arellano, J. P. (1985).

4.3 The Pinochet Regime: From Eclectic Corporatism (Draft Pension Law of 1975) to a Privatized Pension System (DL 3,500 of 1980)

The military regime gave priority to reduce the burden posed by social security outlays on public finances. Some benefits were reduced and eligibility criteria tightened, affecting mainly low-income groups and the middle class. In 1974 a minimum pension for the elderly was established and minimum pensions and family allowances were unified.

In 1975 a basic pension (pension asistencial, PASIS) was established in the middle of a big economic slump driven by shock treatment to reduce inflation along with a deterioration in terms of trade. As a consequence, GDP fell by more than 12 percent and unemployment reached 20 percent. The PASIS was eligible for individuals over 65 and the disabled above 18, and its level was set at one-third of the minimum pension. A study [12]documents that average pensions fell by 26 percent in real terms between 1974 and 1882.[13]

---

[12] Arellano, (1985).

[13] The real value of pensions and real wages declined sharply in the last quarter of 1973, as the inflation rate reached nearly 70 percent in October 1973, following the elimination of most price controls adopted by the military junta.

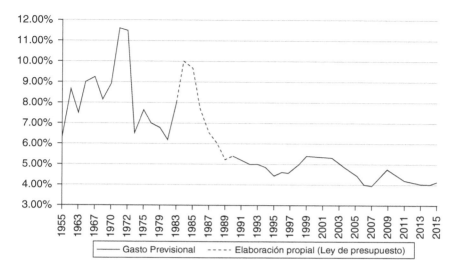

Figure 4.1. Public Expenditure in Pensions, 1955–2015 (Percentage of GDP)

Source: Own elaboration with data from Arellano (1985) and Dipres. The section of the series that includes 1983 to 1989 was based on an assigned budget.

4.3.1 Corporatists and Neoliberals

In July 1974 Augusto Pinochet appointed General Nicanor Diaz-Estrada from the air force as Minister of Labor and Social Security. This general had been active in organizing the military coup against President Allende. Nonetheless, Diaz-Estrada held corporatist views different from the free market orthodoxy of the Chicago economists.[14] In his youth, Diaz-Estrada was a follower of Carlos Ibanez del Campo and a member of the Movimiento Nacionalista Sindical Revolucionario (MNSR), a workers' movement created in 1952 shaped by the ideas of the Spanish Falange during the Franco regime. In the initial years after the coup, Diaz-Estrada convened several labor union leaders from the public sector union (ANEF), the copper sector (CPCH), the trade union of the maritime sector (Confederacion de Trabajadores Marítimos). These unions had opposed the Allende government under the umbrella of the "Poder Gremial"

---

[14] The prominence of the air force in the Ministry of Labor and Social Security lasted until 1976. Then appointed labor ministers were individuals sympathetic to free market ideas. In 1977 General Gustavo Leigh, one of the four-man military junta that launched the coup of September 11, 1973, was deposed along with a group of air force generals by General Pinochet because of discrepancies in the permanence of the military in the government and the excessive personal power acquired by Pinochet.

(guild power). In contrast, the Central Unica de Trabajadores, CUT, the largest labor confederation that had actively supported the Unidad Popular government, was declared illegal after the military coup and its leaders arrested or sent into exile. The corporatists envisaged (non–left wing) trade unions to play a role of intermediation between the military regime and the working class. Conversely, the Chicago-Harvard economists pushed for the complete marginalization of the labor unions (of any ideological sign) in the process of making labor laws and reforming social security.[15]

In November 1975 a draft of pension law was prepared entailing a complete overhauling of the existing pension system. This was called the "Anteprojecto del Estatuto Fundamental de Principios y Bases del Sistema de Seguridad Social."[16] This document was the joint work of the Superintendence of Pensions (SPS) dependent of the Ministry of Labor and Social Security and ODEPLAN, the national planning office in which the Chicago economists had more influence.

The main features of the proposed pension law can be summarized as follows:

(I)   The enrollment in the social security system is compulsory, and the state has the final responsibility of guaranteeing social security benefits to the population (an ILO principle).

(II) Universal coverage for workers in the private and public sectors and the self-employed (ILO principle).

(III) Uniformity of benefits for equivalent contributions (ILO principle).

(IV) Creation of *individual accounts* recording contributions and returns from investments of pension funds in capital markets.

(V)   Pension benefits indexed to inflation.

(VI) The new pension system would be structured around Corporaciones de Seguridad Social (CSS, Social Security Corporations). These are not-for-profit entities, managed by the workers/affiliates and regulated by the state through the Superintendence of Pensions. The CSS would accumulate a reserve fund.

(VII) Free choice among affiliates among Social Security Corporations that would administer the funds of social security.

(VIII) The financial model of the new social security system would combine pay-as-you-go and capitalization funding modalities.

---

[15] The courting, in the initial years of the Pinochet regime, of those labor leaders not in jail included invitations for them to attend the official May 1 celebrations and paid trips to the annual ILO meetings in Geneva, Switzerland.

[16] Anteproyecto, (1975).

(IX) A contributory rate of 10 percent for pensions and 3 percent for severance payments. A real rate of return of 4.5 percent per year (above inflation) was projected. The pension funds in the individual accounts would grow, in real terms, at this rate.

(X) The new system defines a set of *regimenes de prestaciones* (range of benefits) including: (a) pensions, severance payments for job separations, credit to members and (b) a set of health services (*medicina social*), welfare, family allowances, credit and unemployment benefits.

(XI) The system would ensure "sufficient pensions" after retirement; say a reasonable continuity between pensions and last salaries (adequate replacement ratio). The sufficient pension goal is supported by a National Solidarity Fund.

(XII) Pension benefits (old age, disability and survivors) and severance payments would be financed by *private capitalization*.

(XIII) Social health, social welfare benefits, family allowances and other benefits are funded through a *pay-as you-go* modality with a redistributive component (higher-income contributors pay proportionally more to finance the benefits of low-income individuals).

(XIV) Retirement age of 65 for men and 60 for women.

(XV) Special regimes for hazardous jobs and heavy work are maintained.

(XVI) The new social security system will respect the entitlement benefits of the prevailing social security system.

The draft pension law—the *Anteproyecto* report of 1975—was an eclectic synthesis between Bismarck and ILO-based social security principles, with a new financial engineering twist embedded in the individual accounts and capitalization formulas. Moreover, the report contained overly optimistic simulations of replacement ratios in which pensions would be between 85 percent and 130 percent of the last salary for a person contributing for 35–40 years.[17] As shown in the next chapter, these projected replacement rates differ considerably from the *actual* pension/wage ratios delivered by the privatized system.

At the end this draft pension law did *not* prevail. The clout of the corporatist wing in the government that had pushed for adopting (restricted) ILO principles and the workers-managed CSS lasted until 1976. In that year General Diaz-Estrada left the Ministry of Labor and Social Security, being replaced by Minister Sergio Fernandez, who was more sympathetic to the views of the free marketeers.[18]

---

[17] See Anteproyecto, (1975: 12–13)

[18] Diaz-Estrada eventually became a dissident of the Pinochet regime and voted "No" in the plebiscite of 1988, say, against the continuity of the military regime.

The new pension system pushed by the Harvard-Chicago economists discarded ILO principles of tripartite contributions, workers' participation, adequacy of pensions and defined benefits rules. Further, any trace of administration by workers and the trade unions was purged. Social security corporations were replaced by private capitalization managed by *for-profits* pension fund firms. This was in line with the "seven modernizing reforms" of the Pinochet government that included, besides the privatization of social security, a new labor code that severely reduced the actions and scope of labor unions, the privatization of a large part of the education and health systems, the creation of a market of water rights and other neoliberal reforms.[19]

Harvard-trained economist José Piñera Echeñique arrived at the Ministry of Labor and Social Security in late 1978. He led the new labor code and privatized the pension system. The labor code was instrumental to structurally weaken and demobilize the labor movement on a legal basis, avoiding to some extent the use of physical repression to keep workers quiet. In addition, the private pension system would secure a steady flow of cheap funding to big business.

The new pension system was based on the following main principles and modes of operation:

(a) A dominant individual account pillar with compulsory membership for new entrants to the labor force holding legal contracts. Workers could also choose to remain in the old *cajas* or open an account with an AFP and enjoy a cut in contributions. The contribution rate at the AFP was set at 10 percent plus fees, lower than the old *cajas*. Employers were exempted of paying social security contributions (zero contribution rate).

(b) Pension funds could be invested in stocks, bonds issued by commercial companies, the treasury and the central bank. In the new scheme, the Chilean State was *not* authorized to set up a fund management company (e.g. a state-AFP) following the doctrine of the "Estado Subsidiario" (minimal state) embedded in the constitution of 1980.

(c) The AFP system would be regulated by a "Superintendence of AFP" on investments of pension funds, risk factors, capital requirements and so on.

---

[19] Solimano, A. (2012a) and (2015).

(d) Past contributions, rights and entitlements of the old pension boards would be recognized by the state for those choosing the new AFP. A Bono de Reconocimiento (state-issued bond recognizing past contributions to the old *cajas*) was issued.

(e) The Instituto de Normalización Previsional (INP) was created as a body in charge to manage financial flows of the old *cajas*. Nearly 85 percent of pensions paid by INP corresponded to the Servicio de Seguro Social (SSS), la Caja de Empleados Públicos y Periodistas (EMPART) y la Caja de Empleados Particulares (CANAEMPU).[20]

(f) Members of the army, navy, air force, Carabineros, investigative police and Gendarmeria were *exempted* from entering the new capitalization system of the AFP and remained in CAPREDENA and DIPRECA.

4.4 The Military Entertains Doubts on the Privatization Scheme and Remain in Their Old State-Funded System

The new pension law was discussed by the military junta and the *Comité Asesor Presidencial* (General Pinochet's advisory committee composed of military men). These two bodies entertained doubts on the convenience of privatizing social security as recommended by Jose Piñera, labor minister and the economic

---

[20] Old *cajas* remaining in the INP included:
- SSS: Servicio de Seguro Social
- Canaempu: Caja Nacional de Empleados Públicos y Periodistas
- Empart: Caja de Previsión de Empleados Particulares
- Bancaria: Caja Bancaria de Pensiones, Sección de Previsión del Banco Central de Chile, Caja de Previsión y Estímulo del Banco de Chile
- Cajaferro: Caja de Retiro y Previsión Social de los Ferrocarriles del Estado
- Camuval: Caja de Previsión Social de los Empleados Municipales de Valparaíso
- Caprebech: Caja de Previsión y Estímulo de los Empleados del Banco del Estado de Chile
- Capremer: Caja de Previsión de la Marina Mercante Nacional Sección Oficiales y Empleados y Sección Tripulantes de Naves y Operarios Marítimos
- Capremusa: Caja de Previsión de los Empleados Municipales de Santiago
- Capresomu: Caja de Previsión Social de los Obreros Municipales de la República
- Emos: Caja de Previsión de los Empleados y Obreros de la Empresa Metropolitana de Obras Sanitarias, Departamentos de Empleados y Departamento Obreros
- Gasco: Sección de Previsión Social de los Empleados de la Compañía de Consumidores de Gas de Santiago
- Gildemeister: Caja de Previsión Gildemeister
- Hípica: Caja de Previsión Social de la Hípica Nacional
- Hoschild: Caja de Previsión de los Empleados de Mauricio Hotschild
- Salitre: Caja de Previsión para Empleados del Salitre

team. They were skeptical of granting the management of the pension funds to private for-profit companies (a practice with no international precedents at that time), and they were also concerned about the adequacy of the pensions that would pay the new system to those who come into retirement.

Box 4.2 Secret Legislative Session by the Military Junta to Introduce the Capitalization System (Act 398-A)

On October 14, 1980, a *secret* legislative session of the military junta took place to discuss the proposed new pension law. After extended discussions the junta approved the law-decree DL 3,500 that created the AFP system. The decree was published in the *Diario Oficial* (newspaper conveying laws and official decrees) on November 13, 1980. According to Act 398-A, now declassified, the session was attended by General Augusto Pinochet (Army), Admiral Jose T. Merino (navy), General Fernando Matthei (air force) and the General-Director of Carabineros, General Cesar Mendoza (junta members). Several cabinet members and an array of high officers of the armed forces also participated in that session. Minister of Labor and Social Security José Piñera presented his privatization scheme for the pension system. The different junta members voiced some concerns on the proposal but ultimately supported the proposed reform. General Pinochet expressed his doubts on the convenience that the private sector would properly administer a high volume of financial resources belonging to wage earners. Pinochet cautioned that irregularities could occur and mentioned that he was not pleased by the surfacing of "new millionaires" alongside the implementation of the economic model adopted by his regime and indicated that this tendency might be reinforced with the proposed private pension system. He wanted to avoid the creation of "a factory of new millionaires" out of the management of people's pension funds.

He also voiced concerns that funds of the social security could be taken outside Chile (capital flight), losing the hard-won savings of the population. Pinochet asked Jose Piñera to regulate the new managers of the pension fund companies and suggested that the central bank should oversee this reform. Minister Piñera explained the private fund management corporations (AFPs) would not own these funds, just manage them charging a commission "to cover administration costs," downplaying the profit component involved. Priority would be given to investing in low-risk assets such as mortgage letters of credit, government T-bills and central bank bonds subject to diversification criteria (initially investment in stocks would be avoided). To the doubts of placing the private sector in charge of pension fund administration, Minister Piñera suggested that a "capitalization system managed by state entities would be a disaster: if that were the case, better not to reform the current (pension) system." Despite the existing doubts from the legislative session of the military junta, it was agreed to go ahead with the creation of a pension system around individual account system run by commercial companies.

However, the proposed law was intended for the *civilian* population and did *not* apply to members of the national defense system. Pinochet was apprehensive about the contradictory signal that would be given by the military that on one hand approve the adoption of a private capitalization system, but on the other hand did not enroll themselves in the new system, preferring to remain in the *cajas* of CAPREDENA and DIPRECA. Piñera suggested that in five years (to be completed in 1986) the National Defense should join the new capitalization scheme.

Source: National Congress Library, Act 398-A of the Military Board, 1980.

4.5 Concluding Remarks

Since the mid-19th century, Chile has put in place different mechanisms of social insurance and social security protection in response to social demands and changing economic development processes. After a slow start, new labor laws were passed in a rush of legislation in 1924–25, pressed by a military uprising and the growing strength of the workers movement. Between the 1940s and the early 1970s, social spending, including pension outlays, expanded significantly as share of national income. The social security system built in that period embedded principles of intergenerational solidarity and progressive redistribution. Nonetheless, its operation was also affected by fragmentation of rules, absence of full indexation to inflation, shortages of fiscal revenues, lack of coverage of women, the self-employed and rural workers and overall systemic complexity. Various governments of different ideological persuasions (Gonzalez Videla, Ibañez del Campo, Frei and Allende) attempted reforms of the system addressing these problems while expanding benefits to more vulnerable groups. Effective reform, however, was difficult to attain. After the military coup of September 1973, the dominant concern of the military and its economic advisors was reducing the fiscal burden of the social security system. Although some targeted benefits were set at modest levels to counteract the effects of the shock treatment policies applied in the mid-1970s, there was an overall tendency of cutting benefits to the working class and middle-income groups, shielding the military from these cuts. After an initial attempt of overhauling the pension system along corporatist lines with workers administering pension funds supervised by the state, neoliberal reform prevailed in the early 1980s, leading to pension privatization for the civilian population. Traditional criteria and principles of social security recommended by the International Labor Office were eschewed in favor of notions of individual responsibility and a strong urge to introduce individual pension accounts and create a domestic capital market became the priority. At the same time the consolidation and formation of new economic conglomerates were favored through the channeling of the pension funds generated by wage earners to large firms and big capital.

Annex

Table A.4.1. Labor and Social Security Legislation in Chile (1832–1979)

Year of Approval or Creation	Law or Decree	Name/Purpose	Brief Description	Source	Source of Number of Law
1832	-	Central Charity and Public Health Board	Supervision of charities and health policy.	(13)	-
1855	-	Military *montepio* Law	*Montepío* is a pension right to widows and orphans.	(14)	(14)
1858	Ley S/N	Savings Board of Public Employees (Caja de Ahorros de Empleados Públicos)	First social security body established in Chile.	(8)	(8)
1865	-	Industrial relation law (Commercial Code)	Regulations of job relations between employers and workers.	(16)	(8)
1888	-	Mining Code			

Year of Approval or Creation	Law or Decree	Name/Purpose	Brief Description	Source	Source of Number of Law
1906	1,838	Workers' housing Law (Ley de habitaciones obreras)	Promotes the access to low-cost housing for workers.	(2)	(3)
1907	1,990	Sunday Holiday Law (Ley Descanso Dominical)	Mandatory for women and children under 16.	(8)	(8)
1911	2,498	Savings Board of Railroad Workers (Caja de Ahorros de Empleados de Ferrocarriles del Estado)	Funded by mandatory contributions from workers, employees and employers.	(8)	(8)
1912	2,675	Child Protection Law	Limits child labor under eight years old. Fines/imprisonment for hiring children performing heavy and hazardous jobs, and nightlife paid-work.	(8)	(8)
1914	2,951	Protection Law for workers in the commerce sector (Ley de la silla)	Allows temporary resting of commercial employees. Provision of chairs for sitting and lunch break.	(1)	(3)
1915	3,029	Pension and *Montepío* Board for the army and navy	-	(3)	(3)
1916	3,170	Compensation payment for work accidents	For blue-collar and white-collar workers.	(1)	(3)
1917	3,321	Reform to Sunday Holiday Law	This law applies for workers of all age (men and women).	(3)	(3)
1917	3,186	Nursery Law (Ley de Salas cuna)	Applies to companies with more than 50 female workers over 18 years old. It allows female workers one hour per day devoted to breastfeed.	(1) (2)	(8)

(*continued*)

Table A.4.1. (*cont.*)

Year of Approval or Creation	Law or Decree	Name/Purpose	Brief Description	Source	Source of Number of Law
1918	3,379	Pension Board of Railworkers (Caja de Retiros y de Previsión Social de los Ferrocarriles del Estado)	-	(3)	(3)
1923	3,915	Law Regulating Heavy Work	Sets a maximum of 80 kg per bag to be carried by a worker.	(1)	(8)
1924	4,053	New Labor Contract Law	It establishes an 8-hour working day, banning child labor, regulates women's work in heavy and hazardous activities.	(5)	(8)
1924	4,053	General Labor Directorate (Dirección General del Trabajo)	Gathers and publishes all information related to labor activities and compliance with social and labor laws.	(10)	(10)
1924	4,054	Mandatory Social Insurance for manual workers (Caja del Seguro Obrero Obligatorio – CSO)	Social insurance for blue-collar workers. Granting sick-medical assistance, dental care, death, and disability and retirement pensions.	(7)	(7)
1924	4,057	Trade Union Law (Ley de Organización Sindical)	Legal recognition of industrial and professional unions. It allows profit-sharing schemes with trade unions.	(6)	(8)
1924	4,055	Allowance payment for work accidents and occupational diseases	Employer's responsibility in occupational accidents and diseases.	(4)	(8)

Year of Approval or Creation	Law or Decree	Name/Purpose	Brief Description	Source	Source of Number of Law
1924	4,059	White-collar Labor Law in the Private Sector	Regulates working hours, paid vacations, sick leave, severance payments. It includes mandatory saving programs for white-collar workers.	(6)	(8)
1924	4,056	Law of Conciliation and Arbitration	It establishes conciliation and arbitration judicial courts for collective labor disputes. It recognizes the right to strike by workers.	(6)	(8)
1924	DL 44	Ministry of Labor, Hygiene and Social Welfare		(4)	(6)
1924	DL 188	Pension Board of Private Sector Employees (Caja de Previsión de Empleados Particulares)		(4)	(9)
1925	Constitution	Constitution of 1925	New constitution incorporating progressive labor legislation, protection of civil rights and the "social function of property."	(6)	(6)
1925	DL 454 – DL 767	Pension Board of Public Employees and Journalists (Caja Nacional de Empleados Públicos y Periodistas)	Granting of old age, disability and survivor's pensions. Provision of medical assistance to civil servants and journalists.	(4)	(8)
1925	DL 526	Superintendency of Public Beneficence	Supervision of sanatoriums, orphan houses, lazarettes and cemeteries.	(10)	(10)

(continued)

Table A.4.1. (*cont.*)

Year of Approval or Creation	Law or Decree	Name/Purpose	Brief Description	Source	Source of Number of Law
1925	4,052	Pension Board of Armed Police (Caja de Asistencia, Prevision y Bienestar Social de la Policía)	Insurance of occupational hazards, funeral expenses, medical care, and *montepío* for family members.	(17)	(17)
1931	DFL 178	Unified Labor Code	It integrates previously separated labor laws, sets minimum wages and severance payments for blue-collar and white-collar workers.	(6)	(8)
1936	5,950	Creation of Popular Housing Fund (Caja de Habitación Popular)	Promotion of low-cost, quality housing.	(1)	(8)
1937	6,037	National Merchant Marine Pension Board (Caja de Previsión de la Marina Mercante Nacional)	Insurance of risks of illness, disability, old age and death for employees of National Merchant Marine.	(8)	(8)
1938	6,174	Preventive Health Service	Pension Boards managing health services for their members, preventing chronic and work-related diseases.	(8)	(8)
1941	6,836	Pension Board for Employees of the Racetracks (Caja de Previsión de los Empleados de los Hipódromos)	-	(8)	(8)

Year of Approval or Creation	Law or Decree	Name/Purpose	Brief Description	Source	Source of Number of Law
1942	DFL 32/ 1552	National Health Service of Employees	Provision of health services for white-collars workers. Caja Nacional de Empleados Públicos y Periodistas, Caja de Previsión de Empleados Particulares, Caja de Previsión del Personal de la Marina Mercante Nacional, Caja de Retiro y Previsión Social de Empleados Municipales de la República, Caja de Previsión de la Mutual de la Armada y del Departamento de Previsión de la Caja de Crédito Agrario.	(8)	(8)
1946	8,569	Pension board for employees of banks and credits institutions (Caja Bancaria de Pensiones)	For employees of Superintendencia de Bancos, Banco Central de Chile, a la Caja Nacional de Ahorros, a la Caja de Crédito Hipotecario, a los Bancos Comerciales, a los Bancos Hipotecarios, al Instituto de Crédito Industrial y a la Caja Bancaria de Pensiones.	(8)	(8)
1952	10,383	National Social Security Service (Servicio de Seguro Social)	Replaces *Caja de Seguro Obrero* (CSO) for blue-collar workers. The previous capitalization regime of CSO is replaced by PAYG scheme. Centralization of payments of pensions for old age, disability, survivors and funeral aid.	(1) (4)	(8)

(continued)

Table A.4.1. (*cont.*)

Year of Approval or Creation	Law or Decree	Name/Purpose	Brief Description	Source	Source of Number of Law
1952	10,383	National Health Service (Servicio Nacional de Salud)	Integrates numerous services previously dispersed: preventive medicine and medical, maternity, and dental attention for the insured and his family. It covers contributory and noncontributory workers and their families.	(1)	(11)
1953	DFL 245	Family allowance for blue-collar workers (Asignación familiar para los obreros)	Entitlement for contributing workers of the Social Security Service, granted for spouses and children.	(1)	(8)
1953	DFL 243	Unemployment subsidy for workers	Entitlement for contributing workers of the Social Security Service.	(1)	(8)
1953	11,462	Maternity Protection Law	Female employees and workers are entitled to rest six weeks before and six weeks after childbirth, receiving a subsidy.	(1)	(8)
1953	DFL 219	Superintendency of Social Security (Superintendencia de Seguridad Social)	Public agency responsible for collecting information and supervising all social security institutions.	(12)	(8)
1954	D 58	Injury and Disability Regulation of Police (Carabineros)	Administration of injuries and disability benefits.	(4)	(8)
1957	DFL 2252	Retirement Board for employees of the State Bank (Caja de Previsión del Banco del Estado)	-	(4)	(8)

Year of Approval or Creation	Law or Decree	Name/Purpose	Brief Description	Source	Source of Number of Law
1966	16,455	Regulation of the Employment Contracts	Covering blue-collar and white-collar workers. Promotes job security. Employers must justify job separation.	(16)	(8)
1967	16,625	Peasant Unionization Law (Ley de Sindicalización Campesina)	Promotes unionization of agricultural workers.	(16)	(8)
1968	16,744	Regulation on work accidents and occupational diseases	Protective regime for blue-collar and white-collar workers.	(15) (16)	(8)
1968	16,781	Curative Medicine Law (Ley de Medicina Curativa)	Free Choice System of medical services to public, private, active or retired employees and their families.	(13)	(8)
1972	17,592	Pension Board for Merchants, Small Industrialists, Transport sector and Self Employed (Caja de Previsión de los Comerciantes, Pequeños Industriales, Transportistas e Independientes)	-	(12)	(8)
1974–1975	DL 446 – DL 869	Basic Pensions Regulation and Non-contributory pensions pilar (Pensiones Asistenciales, PASIS)	DL 446 seeks to regulate and unify the conditions of existing minimum pensions. DL 869 establishes welfare pensions with limits of beneficiaries.	(12) (8)	(12) (8)

(continued)

Table A.4.1. (*cont.*)

Year of Approval or Creation	Law or Decree	Name/Purpose	Brief Description	Source	Source of Number of Law
1979	DL 2448	Reform of Pension Scheme	Harmonization of pension rules across pensions and savings boards. Minimum retirement ages, indexation rules, and others.	(12)	(12)

(1) Arellano, J. P. (1985). *Políticas sociales y desarrollo: Chile, 1924–1984*. Santiago: CIEPLAN.
(2) Yáñez Andrade, J. C. (1999). "Antecedentes y evolución histórica de la legislación social de Chile entre 1906 y 1924." [Historical Evolution and Background of Social Legislation in Chile, 1906-1925]" *Revista de estudios histórico-jurídicos*, no. 21: 203–10.
(3) Álvarez, A. O., and T. M. Poblete. (1924). *Legislación social obrera chilena*. Santiago.
(4) Mesa-Lago, C. (1978). *Social Security in Latin America: Pressure Groups, Stratification, and Inequality*. Pittsburgh: University of Pittsburgh Press.
(5) Yáñez Andrade, J. C. (2008). *La intervención social en Chile y el nacimiento de la sociedad salarial: 1907–1932* [Social Intervention in Chile and the Birth of Wage-Society; 1907-1932]. Santiago: RIL editores.
(6) Lizama Portal, L. (2011). El Derecho del Trabajo chileno durante el Siglo XX. *Revista chilena de derecho del trabajo y de la seguridad social* 2, no. 4: 109–42.
(7) Herrera, A. B. (1992). *Introducción a la seguridad social*. Editorial Jurídica de Chile.
(8) Biblioteca del Congreso Nacional de Chile. (s.f.). *BCN*. Obtenido de https://www.bcn.cl.
(9) Hinojosa Robles, F. (1967). *La Caja de Previsión de Empleados Particulares: Génesis*. [Pension Board of Private Sector Employees: Origins]. Santiago.
(10) Archivo Nacional de Chile. (s.f.). *Archivo Nacional de Chile* [National Archive of Chile]. Obtenido de https://www.archivonacional.gob.cl/sitio/.
(11) Ministerio de Salud. (s.f.). *Hitos de la salud chilena*. Obtenido de https://www.minsal.cl/hitos-de-la-salud-chilena/.
(12) Vargas Faulbaum, H. L. (2018). *Reformas del sistema de pensiones en Chile (1952–2008)*. [[Reforms of the Pension System in Chile (1952-2008)] Santiago: CEPAL.
(13) Cruz-Coke Madrid, R., and F. Lolas Stepke. (1996). "Historia de la medicina chilena." *Anales de la Universidad de Chile*, no. 4.
(14) Ministerio de Guerra de Chile. (1855). *Lei de Montepío Militar*. Santiago.
(15) Biblioteca Nacional de Chile. (s.f.). *Memoria chilena* [Chilean Memory]. Obtenido de http://www.memoriachilena.gob.cl/602/w3-channel.html.
(16) Comisión de Estudios de la Seguridad Social, Chile. (1965). *Informe sobre la reforma de la seguridad social chilena*, volume 2. Santiago: Editorial Jurídica de Chile.
(17) Dirección de Previsión de Carabineros de Chile. (s.f.). *Quiénes somos: Nuestra historia*. Obtenido de https://www.dipreca.cl/historia.

Chapter 5

EMPIRICAL ELEMENTS FOR EVALUATING THE PRIVATIZED CHILEAN PENSION SYSTEM

5.1 Introduction

The focus of this chapter is on the economic and social performance of the privatized pension system in Chile implemented since the early 1980s. To evaluate the pension system we can use several criteria, such as:

a. The value of pensions relative to wages (replacement ratios) or relative to per capita income and the poverty rate.
b. Degree to which the system is balanced in its financing (i.e., tripartite contributions).
c. Differences in pension levels between sub-systems (horizontal equity of benefits).
d. Costs of managing the private pillar. Profit rates of the private pension-management fund companies.
e. Level and composition of public spending to support the overall pension system.
f. Who uses the savings of the pension funds pool, in particular the financing of economic conglomerates, commercial banks, private corporations, export of Chilean wage earners' pension savings to other economies.
g. Workers' participation in the operation and investment policies of the pension funds.
h. Fiscal impacts of the transition from PAYG to capitalization.

In Chile as of the late 2010s, the average pensions paid by the dominant private capitalization pillar (AFP and insurance companies) is the lowest of any pillar (except the *pilar solidario*). It is below the average pensions paid by the pillar of the old *cajas* (IPS) and only represents 20–25 percent of the average pensions paid by the national defense pension system (CAPREDENA and DIPRECA). Other features of the current pension system are: (a) the existence of significant gender-based differences in pension levels, (b) only employees have to make regular contributions to the dominant private capitalization pillar, excepting employers of their contribution, (c) employees have no seats in the board of directors of the pension of the pension-management companies, depriving them of voice and voting power in corporate decisions affecting the pension funds. These practices depart from the social security standards promoted by the International Labor Office and ratified by member countries around the world.

As of 2018 the share of pension funds invested within Chile represents 58 percent of the total pension funds, and 42 percent of the funds are invested *outside* the country. In a nation like Chile with shortage of national savings to support domestic economic development and reduce poverty, inequality and advance environmental goals this practice of exporting abroad a large proportion of pension savings is highly controversial.

The proportion of investment of pension funds allocated inside Chile between the private sector (commercial banks and corporations) and the public sector (chiefly the national treasury and the central bank) is roughly 65:35, underscoring the dominant use of the financial resources accumulated in the pension funds generated by wage earners to finance the investment needs of the corporate sector.

5.2 Average Old Age Pensions Paid by Private and Public Contributory Pillars

The average monthly pension (men and women) paid by the private pillar is close to US$ 300 per month, with little variation between 2016 and 2019. As of mid-2019 the value of the average pension for men was US$ 384 and for women US$ 242, confirming the existence of a significant gender gap in pension payments.

These average monthly pensions are below the minim wage (above US$ 400 in 2019). In addition, average pensions are well below the monthly per capita income of Chile that is slightly above US$ 2,000.[1]

Table 5.1 confirms our assertion that the AFP and insurance companies' private pillar pays the *lowest* average pension among the three contributory pillars. In 2019 the average pension paid by the AFP/insurance companies represents 82 percent of the average pension paid by the IPS (old *cajas*), 21 percent of CAPREDENA's average pension and 19 percent of DIPRECA's

---

[1] This comes from dividing the annual per capita income (US$ 25,000 in 2018, purchasing power parity calculation) by 12 months.

Table 5.1. Monthly average pension of retirement of different pillars (A) (USD of June 2019)

			2016	2019	% Variation
			(1)	(2)	(3)
Private System (AFP and Insurance Companies) (B)	Scheduled Withdrawal (*Retiro Programado* - AFP)	Men	244.3	245.8	0.6%
		Women	153.4	154.3	0.6%
		Average	187.3	188.0	0.4%
	Annuity Payments (*Renta Vitalicia* - Insurance Companies)	Men	503.6	491.3	-2.4%
		Women	437.4	425.6	-2.7%
		Average	469.7	459.7	-2.1%
	(*Renta Temporal* - AFP)	Men	787.6	953.5	21.1%
		Women	872.3	836.7	-4.1%
		Average	836.4	913.0	9.2%
	Average	Men	374.6	385.0	2.8%
		Women	248.9	242.2	-2.7%
		Average	301.4	302.9	0.5%
Old Public System (*Cajas* - IPS)		Men	435.9	458.6	5.2%
		Women	310.7	321.8	3.6%
		Average	352.3	367.3	4.3%
Pension System for the Armed Forces (CAPREDENA) (C)		Men	1,458.8	1,471.4	0.9%
		Women	1,145.9	1,176.2	2.6%
		Average	1,426.9	1,440.6	1.0%
Pension System for National Police and other Services (DIPRECA) (D)		Men	1,530.0	1,586.2	3.7%
		Women	1,646.3	1,652.7	0.4%
		Average	1,540.0	1,592.2	3.4%

Average wage of contributors AFP

		2016	2019	% Variation
Men		1,182.8	1,263.2	6.8%
Women		1,012.8	1,106.5	9.3%
Average		1,111.3	1,196.8	7.7%

(*continued*)

Table 5.1. (*cont.*)

	2016	2019	% Variation
	(1)	(2)	(3)
Ratio Private System Pensions to:			
IPS	86%	82%	−3.6%
CAPREDENA	21%	21%	−0.5%
DIPRECA	20%	19%	−2.8%
Average wage of contributors AFP	27%	25%	−6.7%

A. Column corresponds to data of June 2019. Column 2016 corresponds to November data, except CAPREDENA (October) and DIPRECA (September)

B. Self-funded component without fiscal subsidies. Private pillar pays pensions in three modalities: Retiro Programado (64,6%), Renta Vitalicia (30,7%) and Renta Temporal (4,8%)

C. It includes army, navy and air force

D. It includes National Police (Carabineros), Investigative Police (PDI) and Jail System Staff (Gendarmería)

Sources: Superintendence of Pensions (SP), Statistical office of CAPREDENA, Statistical office of DIPRECA.

average pension (the average for 2016 was roughly similar). Moreover, the ratio of the average pension to average wages paid by the private pillar was 27 percent in 2016 and 25 percent in 2019.

5.3 Frequency Distribution for Old age Pensions Paid by the AFP System

The frequency distribution of old age pensions (average for men and women) paid by the AFP system by income brackets are concentrated at the bottom: over 90 percent are below US$ 246 per month.[2] Only 5 percent of recipients receive a monthly pension above US$ 500 per month, confirming the very skewed distribution to the bottom of the pension distribution. This feature is even more acute for women (Table 5.2).

5.4 Pension Levels for Members of the Armed Forces and National Police

The social security system for the personnel of Chilean National Defense obeys very different rules from the private capitalization system and the old

---

[2] This is equivalent to Ch$ 167,000 in June 2019.

Table 5.2. Frequency Distribution of Monthly Average Old Age Pension (AFP) (June 2019, Current prices USD)

Pensions	Scheduled Withdrawal (*Retiro Programado*)					
	TOTAL		MEN		WOMEN	
	Number of beneficiaries	Percentage	Number of beneficiaries	Percentage	Number of beneficiaries	Percentage
	(1)	(2)	(3)	(4)	(5)	(6)
US$ 123 or less	149,348	32%	59,114	34%	90,234	30%
Between US$ 123 and US $246	279,363	60%	88,642	52%	190,721	64%
Between US$ 246 and US$ 493	18,849	4%	10,057	6%	8,792	3%
Between US$ 493 and $1,724	18,345	4%	11,184	7%	7,161	2%
US$ 1,724 and more	3,150	1%	2,923	2%	227	0%
Total	**469,055**	**100%**	**171,920**	**100%**	**297,135**	**100%**

Source: Superintendence of Pensions (SP)

cajas. This national defense tier is funded in a bi-partite way between the state (employer) and the military personnel (contributors) with the state bearing nearly 90 percent of the pension benefits of national defense; these outlays are paid out of the national state budget. The retirement age in the defense sector is lower than that of the civilian system.[3]

It is worth noting that any analysis of the benefits earned by the armed forces presents the practical problem that the pension and other benefits information collected by CAPREDENA and DIPRECA is *not* regularly published by the Superintendence of Pensions, the Ministry of Defense, the Government Budget Office or the Ministry of Labor and Social Security.[4] The data presented in this book was obtained through a request to pension administration of CAPREDENA and DIPRECA according to provisos of the Chilean transparency law.

Table 5.3 presents information on old age, survivors and disability pensions for CAPREDENA (army, air force and navy) for 2016 and 2019 expressed in real US dollars. Average old age pensions for these two years are over the equivalent of US$ 1,400 for men and US$ 1,145 for women. Survivor pensions are lower than old age pensions but disability pensions are almost equivalent, if not higher. These average pension levels are *five times higher* than those paid by the private capitalization pillar.

Table 5.4 presents data on pension benefits (old age, survivors and disability) paid by DIPRECA in 2016 and 2019. It is worth noting that DIPRECA's average pensions per person are higher than those paid by CAPREDENA (although the number of beneficiaries is lower).

5.5 Incidence of Public Expenditure in the Pension System

The public sector paid, in 2014, nearly 2.4 million pension benefits[5] to the Solidarity Pillar, IPS and National Defense. In turn, the AFP + insurance companies in the private pillar paid pensions to nearly one million people in that year (table 5.4).

In aggregate terms, public expenditure on pensions represents 64 percent of the total, while the AFP and insurance companies contribute only 36 percent of total pension spending (table 5.4). However, the largest number of affiliates by far is enrolled in the capitalization pillar.

---

[3] Retired armed forces officials can be rehired by the armed forces at a salary after retirement.

[4] A partial exception of the generally scant information on the pension system of national defense is a study conducted in 2011 (published in 2012) by the National Budget Office (DIPRES) of the Chilean Ministry of Finance (see Benavides and Jones 2012).

[5] One person can receive more than one pension benefit.

Table 5.3. Monthly Average Pensions of CAPREDENA (Army, Navy and Air Force) (Number of beneficiaries and dollar value, USD of June 2019)

	TOTAL		MEN		WOMEN	
	Number of beneficiaries	Average pension	Number of beneficiaries	Average pension	Number of beneficiaries	Average pension
	(1)	(2)	(3)	(4)	(5)	(6)
October 2016						
Old age pension	64,275	1,426.9	57,726	1,458.8	6,549	1,145.9
Survivors pension (*Montepío*)	36,174	781.8	756	558.6	35,418	786.6
Disability pension	6,161	1,412.4	5,347	1,410.0	814	1,427.8
Total/Average	**106,610**	**1,207.2**	**63,829**	**1,444.1**	**42,781**	**853.8**
June 2019						
Old age pension	64,917	1,440.6	58,142	1,471.4	6,775	1,176.2
Survivors pension (*Montepío*)	35,232	786.8	771	623.6	34,461	790.4
Disability pension	5,926	1,415.1	5,133	1,409.6	793	1,451.0
Total/Average	**106,075**	**1,222.0**	**64,046**	**1,456.3**	**42,029**	**865.1**
% Variation of Avg. Pension						
Old age pension	1.0%		0.9%		2.6%	
Survivors pension (*Montepío*)	0.6%		11.6%		0.5%	
Disability pension	0.2%		0.0%		1.6%	
Total/Average	**1.2%**		**0.8%**		**1.3%**	

Source: Statistical office of CAPREDENA

Table 5.4. Monthly Average Pensions of DIPRECA (National Police (Carabineros), Investigative Police (PDI) and Jail System Staff (Gendarmeria)) (Number of beneficiaries and dollar value, USD of June 2019)

	TOTAL		MEN		WOMEN	
	Number of beneficiaries	Average pension	Number of beneficiaries	Average pension	Number of beneficiaries	Average pension
	(1)	(2)	(3)	(4)	(5)	(6)
September 2016						
Old age pension	34,630	1,540	31,667	1,530	2,963	1,646
Survivors pension	28,091	698	573	529	27,518	701
Disability pension	2,541	1,791	2,217	1,797	324	1,747
Others	1,630	769	540	1,131	1,090	589
Total/Average	**66,892**	**1,177**	**34,997**	**1,524**	**31,895**	**796**
June 2019						
Old age pension	37,714	1,592	34,284	1,586	3,430	1,653
Survivors pension	25,993	722	605	623	25,388	725
Disability pension	3,217	1,683	2763	1,693	454	1,627
Others	1,432	685	30	759	1,402	683
Total/Average	**68,356**	**1,247**	**37,682**	**1,578**	**30,674**	**840**
% Variation of Avg. Pension						
Old age pension	3.4%		3.7%		0.4%	
Survivors pension	3.5%		17.8%		3.3%	
Disability pension	-6.0%		-5.8%		-6.9%	
Total/Average	**5.9%**		**3.5%**		**5.5%**	

Source: Statistical office of DIPRECA.

Table 5.5. Public and private spending on pensions (2014)

	Expenditure 2014 (Millions of Pesos)	Participation in total Expenditure in Pension Benefits	N° of pensions paid[a] (beneficiaries)	% pensions paid
	(1)	(2)	(3)	(4)
Solidarity Pillar	1.095.828	16,70%	PBS: 583.202	23,81%
			APS: 698.426	--------
IPS	1.731.548	26,40%	689.714	28,16%
Armed Forces	1.377.074	21,00%	171.501	7,00%
AFP- Programmed retirement and others	922.738	14,10%	518.249	21,16%
Annuity	1.424.200	21,70%	486.255	19,86%
Total	6.551.388	100%	2.448.921*	100%

NOTES: PBS(*Pension Básica Solidaria*, basic pension), APS (*Aporte Previsional Solidario*, supplementary pension for low income recipients).
* To avoid double accounting it does not include APS.
[a] Includes pensions of old age, disability and montepío, December 2014.
Source: Own elaboration from data by the Budget execution of the IPS, CAPREDENA, and DIPRECA, published by DIPRES. Also, data from the social security statistic sheet published by the Superintendence of Pensions.

The share of public expenditure in the Solidarity Pillar providing benefits to over 1.2 million people in 2014 (column 2 of table 5.4) was 17 percent, while the share of public spending in CAPREDENA and DIPRECA reached 21 percent and provides benefits to 172,000 military personnel and their families. The fact that spending benefiting the armed personnel with an universe of beneficiaries that are only 14 percent of the beneficiaries of the pilar solidario is explained by the significantly higher pensions per beneficiary in the national defense pillar.

International Perspective

In international perspective, the level of public spending in pensions in Chile, as a share of GDP, is less than half of the OECD average, close to 8 percent of GDP (see figure 5.1). The share of public spending in pensions of Chile is only higher than those of Mexico, Iceland and Korea (2011).

5.6 Effects on Savings, Inequality and Level of Pensions

One of the main arguments of the promoters of the capitalization system is its allegedly positive effect in fostering savings mobilization, leading to speedier economic growth. An empirical study by Corbo and Schmidt-Hebbel (2003), using an empirical macroeconomic model, finds that the AFP pension system would have had a positive effect on Chile's GDP growth through a positive net saving effect. Nonetheless, we know that the saving, investment and growth process is complex and subject to multiple causality between these three variables.[6] Therefore it is not easy, realistically, to isolate the specific contribution of the individual account system to the overall growth pattern of a country.

The supposedly positive effect on *national* savings of the compulsory pension savings system (capitalization pillar) has to be examined also considering two effects at work: (a) people subject to compulsory saving may react by reducing their voluntary savings. The relevant impact is the *net* effect on total personal savings. (b) there is a substitution between private and *public savings*. In Chile the transition toward a private capitalization system implied a negative effect on public savings of nearly 3 percent of GDP for around 30 years.[7] This effect reduced the expected positive effect on national savings (which is equal to the sum of private savings plus government savings) of the capitalization system.

For an increase in national savings to accelerate GDP growth, an increase in fixed capital investment has to take place. As Chile is a financially open economy the rise in national savings is not necessarily equal to an increase of the same magnitude in investment: part of the increase in national savings may be offset by a fall in foreign savings (smaller current account deficit in the balance of payments) in economies with a degree of financial integration with the rest of the world.[8] Fuentes (2013) calculates an offset coefficient for investment of nearly 0.5 for Chile.

To evaluate the net effects of the pension system on the population's well-being we must not only look at its impact on GDP but also consider how this system affects the distribution of wealth and income.

Chile is a highly unequal economy. Using income data from the Consumer Financial Survey published by the central bank the calculated income Gini coefficient is around 50 percent, the net wealth Gini is 70 percent and the

---

[6] Solimano and Gutiérrez (2009).

[7] Bravo and Uthoff (1999).

[8] See Feldstein and Horioka (1979) for the seminal study on this effect applied to industrial economies.

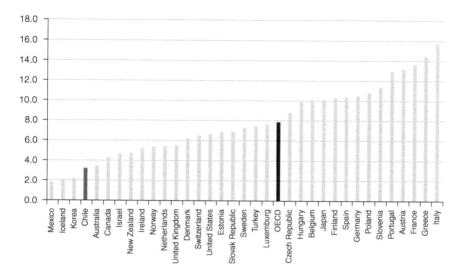

Figure 5.1. Public spending on pensions from OECD countries as a percentage of the GDP (2011)

Source: OECD (2015).

Gini for personal financial assets is 90 percent.[9] Given that the pension system redistributes savings from wage earners to capital owners it contributes to the overall concentration of wealth in the Chilean economy.

Profit Rates of the AFP system

The high profit rates earned by the AFP system have an impact on income distribution. There are three main sources of profits for the AFPs:

(i) *explicit* commissions.
(ii) *implicit* commissions (fees charged to the AFP by investment banks that are deducted from the principal of the affiliate's account) and,
(iii) profits earned on investments of reserve requirements held by the AFP.[10]

According to a study by the Chilean Ministry of Labor and Social Security (Vila, 2014) the value of pensions at retirement can decline by 20–30 percent over a period of three decades due to the deductions of *implicit* commissions.

---

[9] Solimano (2017)
[10] The practice of these implied commissions was apparently authorized by DL 3,500 of 1980 and maintained by the Law 20,225 of 2008.

Table 5.6. Average Rate of Return on equity of AFP System (1) (Ratio of profits on the net equity, percent)

Year	ROE (%)
2004–2018 Average	**22.1%**
2018	10.2%
2017	12.1%
2016	12.7%
2015	22.3%
2014	29.6%
2013	31.4%
2012	26.5%
2011	18.6%
2010	27.2%
2009	32.7%
2008	-0.4%
2007	29.0%
2006	32.0%
2005	22.2%
2004	24.8%

Source: Superintendence of Pensions.

Using data from the Superintendence of Pensions the average profit rate of the consolidated AFP system in the period 2004–18 was 22.1 percent, registering ups and downs through different sub-periods. This very high average rate of profit suggests the existence of supernormal profits in the pension intermediation industry as it bears little resemblance with the productivity of physical capital in the Chilean economy that is calculated (in terms of a social rate of return) to be nearly 8 percent. The existence of super-normal profits suggests the existence of strong barriers to entry to this industry typical of monopolistic or oligopolistic market structures. In fact, the pension management industry has experienced a steady process of market concentration in the past three decades. In the mid-1990s there were 23 AFP operating, some of the them owned and managed by trade unions in the copper sector and schoolteachers. In contrast, as of the late 2010s there are only six AFP in the market, all owned by private companies operating under strictly for-profit criteria.

5.7 How Pension Funds Are Invested?

From the point of view of wealth distribution and the overall savings-investment process, an important dimension is the *use or destination* of the accumulated savings in the pension funds that in Chile represent nearly 70 percent of GDP. By its financial design and regulatory framework the AFP system can invest only in stocks, bonds and other financial instruments issued by financial and non-financial corporations in Chile and abroad and approved by the financial regulator. These instruments are traded in local and international capital markets. As already noted the sector of small- and medium-sized enterprises does not issue stocks and bonds as a mechanism to raise capital to finance their investment plans and working capital; hence, the pension funds cannot invest in these companies. In addition, the AFPs do not engage in directly financing social projects such as public schools and hospitals.

The investment patterns of the AFP system by type of institution are depicted in table 5.7.

Economic conglomerates that have important capital positions in banking, mining, retail, fishing, forestry and other activities largely benefit from access to the pension funds. In fact, the largest family conglomerates (Lucksic, Said, Yarur, Saieh, Matte and others) capture around 25 percent of the total value of pension funds accumulated by the system, roughly US$ 50 billion (table 5.8). This reinforces the point that the use of the pension funds to finance big business and economic conglomerates contributes to the very high wealth concentration at the top in Chile.

Another feature of the pension fund industry is its growing *de-nationalization*. International financial conglomerates, mostly specialized in the insurance sector area, such as MetLife, Principal Financial Group, and Sura Group, control the main share of property of the Chilean pension management companies. These international corporations have their main boards of directors located outside Chile and act as profit-maximizing entities on an international scale. Table 5.9 shows that Principal Financial group (a holding based in the United States) controls over 97 percent of the shares of CUPRUM, an AFP originally created by the trade unions of the copper sector. In turn, MetLife insurance, also established in the United States, controls 95 percent of the capital of the AFP Provida. AFP Capital, controlling nearly 20 percent of the market, is owned entirely by the Colombian-based Sura Asset Management Group. Three foreign-owned AFP—Cuprum, Habitat and Provida—manage 63 percent of the pension fund assets, reaching a total of US$ 133.7 billion in 2019.[11] The only large AFP that is controlled, mostly, by a Chilean investment group is Habitat, which holds 28 percent of total assets of the pension funds industry. The controlling investment group of Habitat is closely linked to the *Camara Chilena de la Construcción* (a home-owners association).

---

[11] Out of US$ 212.860 accumulated in the system (see column 1, table 5.9, data of 2019).

Table 5.7. Investment of Pension Funds (February 2019)

Type of Institution	Value of Pension Funds in Billion US$	% Total of assets	% Total of Pension Funds (under parenthesis, share of investment in Chile)
	(1)	(2)	(3)
Commercial Banks			
Banco de Chile	7,324	16.3%	–
Banco Santander Chile	6,978	15.5%	–
Banco de Crédito e Inversiones	6,371	14.2%	–
Banco Itau-Corpbanca	6,084	13.5%	–
Banco Scotiabank Chile	5,961	13.3%	–
Banco del Estado de Chile	5,570	12.4%	–
Banco Security	2,239	5.0%	–
Banco BICE	2,195	4.9%	–
Banco Falabella	812	1.8%	–
Banco Consorcio	591	1.3%	–
Others	816	1.8%	–
Total	**44,941**	**100.0%**	**21.1% (36.1%)**
State Sector			
General Treasury	39,367	88.4%	–
Central Bank	5,061	11.4%	–
Others	98	0.2%	–
Total	**44,526**	**100.0%**	**20.9% (35.9%)**
Private Corporations (Publicly own S.A.) Top 10 Private Corporations in Chile			
S.A.C.I. Falabella	1,943	6.5%	–
Cencosud S.A.	1,918	6.5%	–
Empresas Copec S.A	1,878	6.3%	–
Latam Airlines Group S.A.	1,666	5.6%	–
ENEL Américas S.A.	1,525	5.1%	–
ENEL Chile S.A.	1,043	3.5%	–
Celulosa Arauco y Constitución S.A.	1,021	3.4%	–
Empresas CMPC S.A.	982	3.3%	–
Colbun S.A.	960	3.2%	–
Empresa de Transporte de Pasajeros Metro S.A	905	3.0%	–

Type of Institution	Value of Pension Funds in Billion US$	% Total of assets	% Total of Pension Funds (under parenthesis, share of investment in Chile)
	(1)	(2)	(3)
Top 10 Corporations	**13,841**	**46.6%**	–
106 other companies	15,862	53.4%	–
Total	**29,703**	**100.0%**	**14.0%**
			(24%)
Investment funds, Mutual Funds*	**5,166**	**100.0%**	**2.4%**
			(4.1%)
Total investment inside Chile	**124,336**	**100.0%**	**58.4%**
Total investment outside Chile	**88,524**	**100.0%**	**41.6%**
Total Pension Funds	**212,860**	-	**100.0%**

*Investment funds, Mutual Funds and Venture Capital Funds
Source: Gálvez, R., & Kremerman, M. (2019).

Main controllers:

- **CAPITAL**
  - o Sura Asset Management Chile S.A.: SURA Group company. Colombian conglomerate with high presence in the insurance sector in Latin America.
- **CUPRUM**
  - o Principal Chile Ltda.: Chilean subsidiary of Principal Financial Group USA, a US financial investment management and insurance company
- **HABITAT**
  - o Inversiones Previsionales Dos SPA: Controlled by *Inversiones La Construcción* (owned in 67% by *Cámara Chilena de la Construcción* (Gálvez, 2017)
  - o Inversiones Previsionales Chile SPA: Controlled by Prudential Chile, a subsidiary of Prudential Financial company, a US financial investment management and insurance company
- **MODELO**
  - o Inversiones Atlántico: Navarro Haeussler family as shareholders
- **PLANVITAL**
  - o Asesorías e Inversiones Los Olmos S.A.: Controlled by *Sociedad de Islas Vírgenes BritánicasAtacama Investments Ltd.*, which is corporately dependent

Table 5.8. Investment of the Pension Funds by Main Chilean Economic Conglomerates, 2019.

Ranking	Economic Conglomerates	Value of Pension Funds in Billions US$	% per Economic Conglomerate
1	Grupo Luksic	$8,956	17.7%
2	Grupo Said	$7,413	14.7%
3	Grupo Yarur	$6,483	12.8%
4	Grupo Saieh	$6,300	12.5%
5	Grupo Matte	$6,056	12.0%
6	Grupo Solari	$5,102	10.1%
7	Grupo Angelini	$3,028	6.0%
8	Grupo Security	$2,327	4.6%
9	Grupo Paulmann	$1,918	3.8%
10	Grupo Ponce Lerou	$795	1.6%
11	Grupo Consorcio	$678	1.3%
12	Grupo Calderón	$577	1.1%
13	Grupo Navarro	$368	0.7%
14	Grupo C.Ch.C.	$307	0.6%
15	Grupo Sigdo	$275	0.5%
16	Grupo Penta	$0,1	0.0%
-	**Total**	**$50,582**	**100.0%**

Source: Gálvez, R., & Kremerman, M. (2019).

on Assicurrazioni Generali S.P.A., an Italian company that is part of one of the largest insurance fund conglomerates in the world (Gálvez, 2017)
- **PROVIDA**
  o MetLife Inc.: MetLife is one of the largest life insurers in the United States, having presence in nearly fifty countries.

5.8 Other Shortcomings

The Chilean pension system is affected by three additional features that can be summarized as follows.[10]

a. *Complexity*: surveys on consumer satisfaction routinely indicate that affiliates to the pension system have a hard time understanding how the system works. This runs from problems to understand monthly statements to the more complex issue of choosing among different pension funds (A to E) ordered by their profiles of return and risk.[11] The task of rebalancing portfolios after changing conditions in financial markets that affect the value of pension funds is far from trivial for an ordinary citizen to perform.

Another complex choice is the modality of retirement payments: scheduled withdrawals versus annuity.

b. *High administration costs.* The pension fund industry, although exhibiting a large degree of market concentration, still has to compete to attract new affiliates. Unlike public social security in which this problem does not arise, in the private model companies have to spend considerable budgets in marketing, sales force, lavish offices and so on. Ultimately these costs are passed to the affiliate who pays a fee to the AFP.

   In an early assessment of the Chilean pension system, MIT professor Peter Diamond, Nobel Prize in Economics (Diamond, 1993) showed the much higher unit costs of the privatized Chilean pension system compared with the state-run social security system in the United States.

c. *Under-insurance.* Another problem of the Chilean pension system is that under existing rules private fund management companies stop paying pensions when the affiliate runs out of funds under the scheduled withdrawal option. This shifts the longevity risk to the affiliate.[12]

d. *Socially Responsible Investment.* The investment criteria of the pension management companies (AFP) follow strictly market-driven, private, profitability criteria. Caring for the respect of workers' rights, environmental protection in the companies they invest is not a common practice of the Chilean AFP system.

5.9 Political Economy and Forced Savings

The privatized pension system is a highly profitable business niche for the companies that enjoy the rights to intermediate pension funds. They earn monopoly rents that do not want to sacrifice. In addition, the corporate sector benefits greatly from its access to big savings pools coming from compulsory pension funds. From an analytical perspective we can distinguish three mechanisms that gives a strongly pro-business bias to the Chilean privatized pension system (Box 5.1):

a. *A forced savings mechanism.* The mandatory savings in the individual accounts and its corresponding transfer to the corporate sector both inside and outside Chile shape a saving-investment mechanism that clearly benefits big capital.

b. *A Legal Monopoly.* The current system is protected by the legal monopoly granted by the Chilean state to the AFP as the sole administrators of

---

[12] After the reforms of 2008 if an affiliate exhausts his balance in the individual account he or she will receive a basic solidarity pension (minimum pension). The annuity choice is not affected by this discontinuity.

Table 5.9. Ownership of Pension Management Companies (AFP) 2019*

AFP	Pension Funds' Assets in Billions US$ (1)	% Share of Total Pension Funds' Assets (2)	Ownership (3)	% Assets, (4)
Capital	$40,783	19.16%	Sura Asset Management Chile S.A.	99.71%
			Other owners	0.29%
Cuprum	$40,145	18.86%	Principal Chile Ltda.	97.97%
			Other owners	2.03%
Habitat	$59,669	28.03%	InversionesPrevisionales Dos SPA	40.29%
			InversionesPrevisionales Chile SPA	40.29%
			Other owners	19.42%
Modelo	$12,136	5.70%	Inversiones Atlántico**	96.14%
			Other owners	3.86%
Planvital	$7,345	3.45%	Asesorías e Inversiones Los Olmos S.A.	86.11%
			Inversiones Las Gaviotas Ltda.	8.21%
			Other owners	5.68%
Provida	$52,781	24.80%	MetLife Inc.***	95.68%
			Other owners	4.32%
Total	$212,860	100%	-	-

*   Columns (1) and (2) correspond to February 2019, Columns (3) and (4) to June 2019
**   Inversiones Atlántico Ltda. (55.57%), Inversiones Atlántico-A Ltda. (17.47%), Inversiones Atlántico-B Ltda. (13.49%), Inversiones Atlántico Norte Ltda. (9.61%)
*** Inversiones Metlife Holdco Dos Ltda. (42.38%), Inversiones Metlife Holdco Tres Ltda. (42.38%),Metlife Chile Inversiones Ltda. (10.92%)
Source: Superintendence of Pensions.

the pillar of individual pension accounts, preventing any systemic competition to the private pillar. This legal benefit prevents other intermediaries, including the state, from entering the industry of pension management.

c. *Lobby Power of the AFP.* The large resources managed by the AFP lobby provide them a high degree of *political influence* on the branches of executive and legislative powers. This operates through multiple channels such as monetary contributions to politicians in their campaigns for public office, the hiring of lobbyists and the mobilization of economists and financial

---

Box 5.1 Mechanisms of Control and Influence of the AFP System

Level	Function	Consequence
A) Macroeconomic (saving-investment process)	Transfer of pension savings to the corporate sector and economic conglomerates.	Concentration of productive wealth. Control of investment by big corporations.
B) Market structure and pillars	AFP monopoly over individual accounts, absence of alternative public pillar.	Absence of systemic choice between pillars. Monopolistic profits for AFP.
C) Mechanisms of public policy influence	Influence over legislators and politicians, lobby, mobilization of experts, publicity through media	Restricted debate. Blocking of systemic reforms.

---

analysts who praise the benefits of the system. The AFP also mobilize a significant budget for commercial publicity spent on newspapers, magazines, radio and television stations, which helps the pension lobby to set the limits on what is admissible to be discussed around pension reform in the mainstream media.

These different mechanisms seem quite effective in maintaining the private capitalization system in place for nearly four decades diffusing the willingness and ability of governments to reform the pension system and neutralizing social movement and academic critics to the system.

Chapter 6

SYNTHESIS AND CONCLUSIONS: REFORM PARALYSIS AND THE ROAD TO DE-PRIVATIZATION

6.1 Introduction

The empirical evidence presented in the previous chapter points to a reality of low pensions for civilians, large differences in benefits across pillars, large gender biases in pension levels, systemic redistribution of pension savings from wage earners to large economic conglomerates, export of nearly half of the pool pension savings, very high return rates for the AFPs and overall informational complexities for the affiliates.

Governments after the end of the Pinochet regime established a non-contributing, floor pension pillar but have, until the time of the writing of this book, refrained from challenging the AFP monopoly over near eleven millions of individual accounts and introducing an alternative pay-as-you-go pillar that could compete with (or replace) the dominant capitalization pillar. However, and in spite of the opposition of the Piñera II government and after strong popular pressure in August 2020, the Chilean parliament approved the withdrawal of 10 percent of pension funds (subject to bottom and upper limits) to cope with the adverse economic effects of covid-19 pandemic. A second withdrawal was also approved by December of 2020. The system seems to be unraveling.

As part of the reform attempts, two Presidential Advisory Commissions on Pension Reform, both headed by economists, were established: the Marcel Commission (2006–8) and the Bravo Commission (2014–15) convened domestic and foreign social security experts, consultants in pension issues and former AFP executives. However, no trade union members and Chilean critics of the capitalization system participated as permanent members of these commissions.[1] In order to come up with a set of recommendations

---

[1] Two think-tanks that for years held a critical position toward the AFP system are CENDA (National Centre for Alternative Development) and the Fundacion Sol, an applied research center specialized in labor market and pension sector analysis.

to government, they held hearings with a relatively broad spectrum of stakeholders, including critics of the system, but the drafting of policy recommendations was made only by commission members.

6.2 The 2008 Reforms under Bachelet I: Creation of a Basic Pension Pillar

The Pilar Solidario operates under a basic pension (Pension Básica Solidaria, PBS) and a supplementary pension subsidy (APS) for individuals receiving modest pensions; this basic pension pillar is funded out of general tax revenues. The Solidarity Pillar is a targeted pension support scheme; it is not a universal benefit system for all residents of a geographical area or for the whole country. To be entitled to receive the PBS/APS the potential beneficiary has to demonstrate shortage of incomes. The PBS is eligible for individuals who are over 65 years old belonging to the lowest 60 percent of the population.[2] Other benefits are a child subsidy and a subsidy for young workers.[3] The reform of 2008 also renamed the Instituto de Normalización Previsional (INP) as the Instituto de Prevision Social (IPS), with some of its functions redefined. The formulation of pension policies was kept—at least at a formal level—at the Secretariat of Social Security at the Ministry of Labor and Social Security. In practice, main decisions on pensions are made at the Ministry of Finance. In turn, the Superintendencia de AFP was renamed as the Superintendencia de Pensions (SPS). A training and education fund of the affiliates of the system (the Fondo de Educacion Previsional, FEP) and the Survey of Social Security (EPS) were created.[4]

In order to boost some more competition and reduce fees in the capitalization pillar a bidding system for *new* affiliates was also introduced. Although this brought a decrease in *explicit* commissions, *implicit* commissions remained. In retrospect, the limited scope of the 2008 reforms is apparent. Important omissions can be identified:

(A) No phasing-out of DL 3,500 established in 1980. The monopoly held by the AFP as the sole managers of the compulsory pension funds pillar remained in place after the 2008 reforms.
(B) No state-run AFP (or equivalent) and a PAYG pillar were created.
(C) No explicit and enforceable criteria of social responsibility in the investment policies of the AFP were introduced.

---

[2] As of 2018, close to six hundred thousand people receive a Basic Solidarity Pension and around seven hundred thousand receive the APS.
[3] The PBS is delivered by the IPS, and the APS is paid through the AFP system.
[4] See Arenas de Mesa et al. (2008).

(D) The 2008 reforms did not contemplate workers' participation in the corporate policies of the AFP. No ceiling on commissions charged by the AFP
were recommended, expecting only that an auctioning of new entrants
would reduce these fees.

(E) The 2008 reforms did not entail any taxation of supernormal profits of
the AFP.

In addition, in a move that expanded further the reach of the AFP system to
non-wage earners, the Chilean parliament approved a proviso, that enlarged
the profit opportunities of the AFP, in which the self-employed, independent
workers and professionals (the *independientes*) would have to enroll, in a mandatory way after a transition period, in the AFP system. This large segment,
including small company owners, self-employed workers, public sector
employees paid honoraria for their work (many times performing the same
functions of regular employees), craftsman, fisherman, cultural workers and
others, could reach up to two million people.

6.3 Reform Proposals under Bachelet II and Piñera II

Under the Bachelet II administration, the Bravo Commission proposed
three "global options" and 58 specific measures to improve the working of
the pension system. Global option (A) incorporated a series of "parametric"
changes (incremental changes) to the current system under the assessment
that on the whole the AFP pension system was "working well". Global option
(B) proposed the creation of a "social security pillar" with a redistributive
component supported by a collective fund with tripartite financing; in addition, this pillar would adopt a system of "notional accounts" of the Swedish
type. Then, Global option (C) proposed to terminate the system of individual
accounts and replace it by a public pension system run by the state.[5] No consensus among the members of the Bravo Commission emerged on a single set
of recommendations to be delivered to the government.

Within the Bachelet II government there were two broad positions on
pension reform, after the Bravo report was published: one pro-reform stance
aimed at reducing the power of the AFP represented by the Ministry of
Labor and Social Security (led by Minister Ximena Rincon). Another more

---

[5] This option was supported only by a foreign member of the commission, the Polish
economist Leokadia Oleziack, professor of economics and business in the University of
Warsaw in Poland.

conservative position, very sensitive to the views of the AFP industry, was held by the Ministry of Finance (led by Minister Rodrigo Valdes) that wanted only very limited reforms. At the end President Bachelet supported the Finance Ministry view and presented to parliament a draft law introducing a 5 percentage points in contributions by employers (gradually over time). It also proposed the creation of a public pension council administering part of the revenues coming from the employer's contributions.

The Piñera II government (2018–21) as of 2020 has stood for a pension reform package that maintains the current AFP system but seeks to provide more resources to the solidarity pillar keeping the target to the 60 percent poorest segment of the population and makes employers to contribute to overall pension revenues in a gradual way. The reform aims that no pensioner over 65 will fall below the monetary poverty line, adds some benefits for the middle class and women, and provides new subsidies for the older age population. How this will be accomplished remains an open question.

6.4 De-privatizing the Chilean Pension System

It is apparent that after nearly four decades with a privatized pension system, its structural difficulties will hardly be corrected by "parametric" (marginal) policy adjustments as intended by the various governments. Only recently, in May 2020, a group of senators and representatives (*diputados*) in Chilean parliament presented a constitutional reform to eliminate DL 3,500 and create a PAYG system that would replace the AFP system.

A new pension system that will enjoy social legitimacy has to overcome the current privatizing logic. The citizenship wants a pension system that incorporates principles of intrageneration and intergeneration solidarity, a balanced financing structure of social security, the replacement of defined benefits for defined contributions, a level of pension benefits that meet sufficiency criteria, workers' participation, gender equality, financial sustainability and social dialogue. Chile must leave behind the capture of the ample savings pool of social security by financial conglomerates.

In recent years there has been several proposals for more significant reform, including the B and C global options of the Bravo Commission already mentioned and the adoption of a pay-as-you-go system as proposed by the Workers Movement No More AFP.[6] To contribute to the debate, we present here the basic contours of what could be an alternative system for Chile, without venturing into the complex details of its operation.

---

[6] See National Coordination Workers No + AFP (2019).

Contours of a New Pension System

It is important to consider the *initial conditions* of an extremely privatized system operating under a debilitated regulatory framework without a large existing public pillar to the dominant individual accounts. The only existing public pillar besides the Solidarity Pillar is the one managing the pension payments of those who decided to remain in the old *cajas* existing before 1981. An overriding principle must be reestablishing social security as a social right rather than a financial mechanism and business niche.

We can identify two legal reforms required to start a process of *de-deprivatization* of the current system: (i) revocation of the Decree of Law 3,500 that ensures the monopoly of pension funds management to the AFPs, and (ii) *freedom of de-affiliation* from the capitalization pillar so that the citizens can choose among broader alternatives. As shown in chapter 4, when the parliaments of Argentina, Hungary and Poland (between 2008 and 2014) decreed freedom of de-affiliation from the private pillar, their countries' social security began its process of de-privatization.

We can envisage a new pension system built around three pillars:

(i)   *An enhanced Basic Solidarity Pillar* adequately funded and providing *universal and adequate benefits*, overcoming the prevailing logic of targeting of the current system.

(ii)   *Creation of modern pay-as-you-go pillar* operating under well-defined benefits rules linking the pension with the years of contribution and last wages. The funding rules should be based on tripartite contributions following principles of intergenerational and intragenerational solidarity.

(iii) *Demonopolized Pillar of Voluntary Individual Accounts*, a private, nonmandatory, pillar of individual accounts may supplement the pensions paid by the PAYG system, but this segment should be subject to effective competition, without the monopoly of the AFP on the individual accounts.

Basic Solidarity Pillar

The new Solidarity Pillar should have an adequate budget and a logic of universal rights. The level and coverage of the PBS (Basic pension) should be increased and expanded. Its current value is around US$ 150 but the minimum wage is closer to US$ 400. The PBS should approach the level of the minimum wage and its coverage extended from the poorest 60 percent (the current practice) to 100 percent of the population in line with principles of universality and administrative simplification. Another benefit, the cashing of the bonus per child, should coincide with the age of retirement for women (currently women retire at 60 years of age, but they must wait until 65 to cash the bonus).

Public Pay-As-You-Go Pillar

A second pillar would be PAYG that can be managed by a strengthened Institute of Social Security (ISS), properly endowed with the necessary financial and human resources and a broad political commitment from the Chilean state in order to reach this goal. The ISS, in coordination with the National Treasury, would perform the roles of collection and payments of social security benefits. The pillar would be based on a tripartite contribution scheme financed by: (i) employers (companies), (ii) affiliates and (iii) the state. Its coverage would be basically decided by the choice made by citizens between joining the public PAYG pillar or remaining in the private capitalization pillar.[7] As in other countries that have de-privatized their pension system (see Chapter 4), the switch to the PAYG public pension pillar would be accompanied by a transfer of the balances in the individual accounts to the Pension Reserve Fund (PRF).

A PRF already exists in Chile and has (2019) an outstanding stock of nearly $9 billion. Currently the balances of the PRF are managed by the central bank as a fiduciary agent and its surplus invested abroad earning a rate of return. The flow of earnings stemming from these investments can be transferred to the PAYG pillar to enhance its resource base to pay better pensions. The Chilean parliament should consider passing a law ensuring the pension paid by the PAYG should not be lower than the AFP pension in the previous system. The employer's contribution should go to the PAYG pillar that would operate under a *defined benefits rule* and pensions would be calculated following adequacy of benefits criteria as recommended by the International Labor Office. In line with developed countries' practices, benefits besides, being indexed to inflation, would be gradually adjusted over time in response to changes in demographic trends, productivity and life expectancy changes.[8]

---

[7] In option B from the Bravo Commission, it is proposed an equal distribution (50/50) between the PAYG pillar and the capitalization pillar. An alternative procedure is that citizens, according to their preferences, decide the proportions of resources going to both pillars.

[8] In developed countries, benefits are calculated according to two main criteria: (i) points systems (using years of contributions, for example) and (ii) "notional" or fictitious accounts; see Borsch-Supan (2004).

Drawing on the international experience of countries that have de-privatized their pension systems in the last decade around 80–85 percent of the affiliates tend to choose the PAYG when given the choice to select between a public pension pillar and a private pension pillar. Nevertheless, the volume of resource transferred to the public pillar may be lower in relative terms than the percentage of individuals that shift pillars since individuals with higher income and larger balances in the individual accounts may prefer staying in the capitalization pillar (see Chapter 5).

Demonopolized and Voluntary Pillar of Individual Accounts

The third component of the proposed reformed system would be a downsized pillar of individual accounts open to new intermediaries, including nonprofit organizations. The current monopoly of the AFP on the capitalization pillar would end and enrollment to this pillar would be *voluntary*. Additionally, the investment of those funds would not only consider conditions of private profitability, but these investments would respect ethic and social criteria that effectively respect workers' rights, local communities and the environment, and do not engage in illegal practices of making political contributions for lobby purposes. The state would also be allowed to open a pension fund management company under the modality of individual accounts subject to investment rules that ensure a rate of return for account holders, respecting social responsibility and environmental criteria for its investments.

Schemes of voluntary savings tied to pension accounts would be maintained but current tax exemptions should be reviewed. In line with the practices of other countries, collective pension contracts with private or public providers would be stimulated. Three additional topics for a comprehensive reform agenda in Chile should include tackling the challenges posed by: (i) the pension system of the armed forces and Carabineros, (ii) raise women's pensions and (iii) ensure effective pension schemes for independent workers and the self-employed. The de-privatization of the Chilean pension system would require building strong public support for a new public system given the wide social resistance to the privatized system. However, the power of the AFP lobby and its entrenched connections with the political system should not be underestimated. Further, de-privatizing the pension system will strengthen social protection and redirecting savings away from the corporate sector and economic conglomerates triggering important changes in the prevailing neoliberal development model that rests on the use of wage-earner pension savings to cement the concentration of ownership in economic elites.

REFERENCES

Alvarez Andrews, O., and M. Poblete Troncoso. (1924). *Legislación social obrera chilena.*[Social Labor Laws in Chile] Imprenta Santiago, Santiago, Chile.www.memoriachilena.cl.

Archivo Nacional de Chile. (s.f.). *Archivo Nacional de Chile.* [Chilean National Archives] https://www.archivonacional.gob.cl/sitio/.

Arellano, J. P. (1985). *Políticas Sociales y Desarrollo: Chile, 1924–1984.*[Social Policy and Economic Development in Chile, 1924–1984], Santiago: CIEPLAN.

Arenas de Mesa, A., P. Benavides, L. González, J. L. Castillo. (2008). *La Reforma Previsional Chilena: Proyecciones Fiscales 2009–2025* [Chilean Pension Reform: Projections 2009–2025]. Ministerio de Hacienda, Dirección de Presupuestos, Gobierno de Chile.

Biblioteca del Congreso Nacional de Chile. (s.f.). *BCN.* Obtenido de https://www.bcn.cl.

Barr, N. (2000). "Reforming Pensions: Myths, Truths and Policy Choices". *IMF Working Paper*/00/139, Washington, DC.

Barriga, F., M. Kremerman, R. Galvez, B. Saez, F. Gallegos (2020) "Nuevo Sistema de Pensiones para Chile: Modelamiento Actuarial de la Propuesta de la Coordinadora No + AFP" [A New Pension System for Chile: Actuarial Modelling of the Proposal of the No +AFP Movement], Documento de Trabajo, Fundacion Sol, Santiago, Chile.

Benavides, P. y I. Jones. (2012). "Sistema de pensiones y otros beneficios pecuniarios de las Fuerzas Armadas y de Orden y Seguridad Pública y Gendarmería de Chile: Situación actual y proyecciones fiscales 2012–2015." [Pension Systsem and Pecuniary Benefits of the Armed Forces, National Police and Jail System: Current Situation and Fiscal Projections, 2012–2015], Estudios de Finanzas Públicas, diciembre. Dirección de Presupuesto, Ministerio de Hacienda.

Becker, J. (2016). "Europe's Other Periphery." *New Left Review* 99 (May–June).

Bertranou, F., O. Cetrangolo, C. Grushka and y L. Casanova. (2011). "Encrucijadas en la Seguridad Social Argentina" OIT-CEPAL [Social Security in Argentina at Cross-Roads"]. Documento/Report International Labor Office-Economic Commission for Latin America and the Caribbean , Buenos Aires, Argentina.

Börsch-Supan, A. (2004). "What Are NDC Pension Systems? What Do They Bring to Reform Strategies?" World Bank-RFV Conference, Sandham, Sweden, September 29–30, 2004.

Biblioteca Nacional de Chile. s.f. *Memoria Chilena.* [Annals of Chile] http://www.memoriachilena.gob.cl/602/w3-channel.html.

Bravo, J., and A. Uthoff. (1999). "Transitional Fiscal Costs and Demographic Factors in Shifting from Unfunded to Funded Pension in Chile." Working Paper, *Serie Financiamiento del Desarrollo*, 88, UN-ECLAC, Santiago.

Cetrangolo, O., and y C. Grushka. (2008). "Perspectivas Previsionales en Argentina y su Financiamiento tras la Expansión de la Cobertura." [Argentina's Pension Outlook and its Financing After the Broadening of Coverage] *Serie Financiamiento del Desarrollo*, 205, CEPAL.

Cichon, M. (2004). "Approaching a Common Denominator? An Interim Assesment of ILO and World Bank Approaches on Pensions." ILO Social Protection, Financial, Actuarial and Statistical Paper.

Comisión Asesora Presidencial de Pensiones. (2015). *Informe Final*, [Final Report] , Santiago.

Comisión de Estudios de la Seguridad Social, Chile. (1965). *Informe sobre la reforma de la seguridad social chilena*, [Report on the Reform of the Social Security in Chile] volume 2. Santiago: Editorial Jurídica de Chile.

Coordinadora Nacional de Trabajadores NO + AFP. (2019). "Nuevo sistema de pensiones para Chile," [A New Pension System for Chile] noviembre. Santiago, Chile.

Corbo, V., and y K. Schmidt, -Hebbel. (2003). "Efectos macroeconómicos de la reforma de pensiones en Chile," [Macroeconomic Effects of Pension Reform in Chile] Documento Federacion Internacional de Administradores de Fondos de Pensiones, FIAP, Ciudad de Mexico.

Cruz-Coke Madrid, R. (1996). Historia de la medicina chilena.[History of Medicine in Chile] *Anales de la Universidad de Chile*, no. 4: 163–65.

Diamond, P. (1993). "Privatization of Social Security: Lessons from Chile." NBER *Working Paper Series*, WP 4510.

Diamond, P. A., and P. R. Orzag. (2007). "A Summary of Saving Social Security: A Balanced Approach." In R.A. Pruchno & .A. Smyer (Eds.) *Challenges of an Aging Society: Ethical Dilemmas, Political Issues* (pp. 346–395), Baltimore: Johns Hopkins University Press.

Dirección de Previsión de Carabineros de Chile. s.f. *Quiénes somos: Nuestra Historia* [Who we Are: Our History]. Obtenido de https://www.dipreca.cl/historia.

Esping-Andersen, G. (ed.). (1996). *Welfare States in Transition: National Adaptations in Global Economies*. Sage.

Felstein, M., and C. Horioka. (1979). "Domestic Savings and International Capital Flows." NBER Working Paper 310. Cambridge, MA.

Fulz, E. (2012). "The Retrenchment of Second-tiers Pillars in Hungary and Poland: A Precautionary Tale." *International Social Security Review* 65, no. 3.

Gálvez, R. (7 de junio de 2017). *El "corralito legal": ¿Quién gana cuando las AFP se hacen ricas?* [The "legal freeze", Who Wins when the AFP get Richer?] Obtenido de CIPER Chile: https://ciperchile.cl/2017/06/07/el-corralito-legal-quien-gana-cuando-las-afp-se-hacen-ricas/.

Gálvez, R., and M. Kremerman. (2019). ¿AFP para quién? Dónde se invierten los fondos de pensiones en Chile. [AFP for Whom? Investment Patterns of Pension Funds in Chile] *Ideas para el Buen Vivir*(15). Fundacion Sol.

Geanakoplos, J., O. S. Mitchell and y S. P. Zeldes. (1998). "Would a Privatized Social Securty System Really Pay a Higher Rate of Return?" *NBER Working Papers Series*, WP 6713.

Guardiancich, I. (2010). "Italy. Current Pension System: First Assessment of Reform Outcomes and Output." Country Report, European Social Observatory.

Gutiérrez, M., and y A. Solimano. (2009). "Savings, Investment and Capital Accumulation." In *Handbook of International Development*, vol. I, edited by A. Dutt and J. Ross. Edward Elgar Publishers.

Heller, P. S. (1998). "Rethinking Public Pension Reform Initiatives." *IMF Working Paper/* 98/61.

Herrera, A. B. (1992). *Introducción a la Seguridad Social.* [An Introduction to Social Security] Editorial Jurídica de Chile, Santiago, Chile.

Hinojosa Robles, F. (1924). *La Caja de Previsión de Empleados Particulares: Génesis.* [The Pension Board of Private Sector Employees: Origins] Santiago, Chile. www.memoriachilena.cl.

Hirose, K. (2011). "Hungary" en K. Hirose (editor) *Pension Reform in Central and Eastern Europe, in Times of Crisis, Austerity and Beyond.* International Labor Office, Geneva.

Holzman, R., R. Hinz and y M. Dorfman. (2008). "Pension Systems and Reform Conceptual Framework." *SP Discussion Paper* 0824, World Bank.

Hujo, K., and y M. Kulli. (2014). "The Political Economy of Pension Re-Reform in Chile and Argentina." UNRISD, Working Paper 2014-1.

Kotlikoff, L. J. (1998). "Simulating the Privatization of Social Security in General Equilibrium."In *Privatizing Social Security,* edited by M. Feldstein. University of Chicago Press.

Lizama Portal, L. (2011). El derecho del trabajo chileno durante el siglo XX. [Labor Rights in Chile in the XX Century], *Revista chilena de derecho del trabajo y de la seguridad social* 2, no. 4: 109–42.

Mesa-Lago, C. (1978). *Social Security in Latin America: Pressure Groups, Stratification, and Inequality.* Pittsburgh: University of Pittsburgh Press.

———. (2000). "Estudio comparativo del costo fiscal en la transición de ocho reformas de pensiones en América Latina." [Fiscal Costs in the Transition of Eight Pension Reforms in Latin America: A Comparative Study], Serie *Financiamiento del Desarrollo* 93, CEPAL.

———. (2012). "Reversing Pension Privatization: The Experience of Argentina, Bolivia, Chile and Hungary." ESS Working Paper 44, ILO.

Mesa-Lago, C., and y F. Bertranou. (2015). "Los principios de la seguridad social y re-reforma de pensiones en Chile." [Social Security Principles and Pension Reform in Chile], Estudio para la Comisión Presidencial de Pensiones, Santiago, Chile.

Ministerio de Desarrollo Social (MDS). (2014). "Precios sociales vigentes." [Shadow Prices in Chile] División de Evaluación Social de Inversiones, Santiago, Chile.

Ministerio de Guerra de Chile. (1855). *Lei de Montepío Militar.* [Pension Law of the Military], Santiago, Chile .

Ministerio de Salud. (s.f.). *Hitos de la salud chilena.* [Milestones of Health in Chile], Obtenido de https://www.minsal.cl/hitos-de-la-salud-chilena/.

Minsky, H. P. (2008 [1975]). *John Maynard Keynes.* New York: McGraw-Hill..

Mitchell, O. S., and y S. P. Zeldes. (1996). "Social Security Privatization: A Structure for Analysis." *NBER Working Paper,* WP 5512, Cambridge , MA.

OECD. (2015). *Pensions at Glance,* París.

Ortiz, I., F. Duran-Valverde, S. Urban and V. Wodsak (eds.). (2018). *Reversing Pension Privatization. Rebuilding Pension Systems in Eastern Europe and Latin America.* An International Labor Office Report, Geneva, Switzerland.

Oreziak, L. (2013). "Open Pension Funds in Poland—The Experience with Privatization Process." *International Journal of Management and Economics* 38: 102–22, Maharashtra, India.

———. (2016). Personal Correspondence on the Polish Case of Pension Re-Reform.

Orzag, P. R., and y J. E. Stiglitz. (1999). "Rethinking Pension Reform: Ten Myths about Social Security Systems." Conference Paper "New Ideas about Old Age Security." The World Bank, September 14–15, 1999.

Página 12. (2008). "La vuelta a un sistema solidario," [Return to a solidarity system] David Cofre, y "Motivos para el fin de las AFJP," [Reasons for the end of the AFJP] Sol Torres, 7 de noviembre, Buenos Aires, Argentina.

Pallares-Miralles, M., C. Romero and y E. Whitehouse. (2012). "International Patterns of Pension Provision II. A Worldwide Overview of Facts and Figures,", Social Protection and Labor Discussion Paper 1211, the World Bank.

Palmer, E. (2003). "The Swedish Pension Reform Model: Framework and Issues." OECD.

Rodgers, G., E. Lee, L. Swepston and y J. Van Daele. (2009). *The International Labor Organization and the Quest for Social Justice.* ILO, Geneva.

Sen, A. (2012). *A Theory of Justice.* Harvard University Press, Cambridge, MA .

Solimano, A. (2012a). *Capitalismo a la chilena y la prosperidad de las elites.* Santiago: Editorial Catalonia, SSantiago, Chile.

―――. (2012b) *Chile and the Neoliberal Trap,* Cambridge University Press, Cambridge UK and New York .

―――. (2014) *Economic Elites, Crisis and Democracy.* Oxford University Press, Oxford and New York.

―――. (2015) *Elites, crisis y el capitalismo del siglo XXI.* Fondo de Cultura Económica, Santiago, Chile.

―――. (2016) *Global Capitalism in Disarray. Inequality, Debt and Austerity.* Oxford University Press, Cambridge UK and New York .

―――. (2017) *Pensiones a la Chilena.* Santiago: Editorial Catalonia,.

―――. (2020) *A History of Big Recessions in the Long Twentieth Century.* Cambridge University Press,Cambridge, UK and New York.

Standing, G. (2008). "How Cash Transfers Promote the Case for Basic Income." *Basic Income Studies* 3, no. 1: 1–30.

Superintendencia de Pensiones. (December 1, 2019). *Superintendencia de Pensiones.* Obtenido de http://www.spensiones.cl/portal/institucional/594/w3-channel.html.

Vargas Faulbaum, H. L. (2018). *Reformas del sistema de pensiones en Chile (1952–2008).* [Reforms of the Pension System in Chile (1952–2008)] Santiago: CEPAL.

Vila, J. I. (2014). "Los costos que pagan los cotizantes en el sistema AFP." [Costs Paid by AFP Affiliates] *Nota Técnica* # 1, Subsecretaría de Previsión Social.

―――. (2015). "Antecedentes del sistema previsional chileno." [The Chilean Pension System: Background] *mimeo,* Subsecretaría de Previsión Social, Santiago, Chile.

Voget, T. (2008). "Bismarckian Pension Systems," University of Twente.

World Bank. (1994). *Averting Old Age Crisis.* Washington DC.

Yañez Andrade, J. C. (1999). "Antecedentes y evolución histórica de la legislación social de Chile entre 1906 y 1924." [Historical Evolution and Background of Social Legislation in Chile, 1906–1925]" *Revista de Estudios Histórico-jurídicos,* no. 21: 203–10, Valparaiso, Chile .

Yáñez Andrade, J. C. (2008). *La intervención social en Chile y el nacimiento de la sociedad salarial: 1907–1932.* [Social Intervention in Chile and the Birth of Wage-Society;1907–1932].Santiago: RIL editores.

INDEX

Lightning Source UK Ltd.
Milton Keynes UK
UKHW012248191021
392489UK00001B/67